Tackling financial exclu

An area-based approach

Sharon Collard, Elaine Kempson and Claire Whyley

The POLICY PRESS

First published in Great Britain in June 2001 by

The Policy Press
34 Tyndall's Park Road
Bristol BS8 1PY
UK

Tel no +44 (0)117 954 6800
Fax no +44 (0)117 973 7308
E-mail tpp@bristol.ac.uk
www.policypress.org.uk

Published for the Joseph Rowntree Foundation by The Policy Press

ISBN 1 86134 325 6

Sharon Collard is Research Assistant, **Elaine Kempson** is Professor and Director, and **Claire Whyley** is Research Fellow, all at the Personal
Finance Research Centre, University of Bristol.

The **Joseph Rowntree Foundation** has supported this project as part of its programme of research and innovative development projects,
which it hopes will be of value to policy makers, practitioners and service users. The facts presented and views expressed in this report
are, however, those of the authors and not necessarily those of the Foundation.

Photograph on front cover of Barton Hill, Bristol
Cover design by Qube Design Associates, Bristol
Printed in Great Britain by Hobbs the Printers Ltd, Southampton

Contents

Acknowledgements

We wish to acknowledge the support of the Joseph Rowntree Foundation who financially supported this project.

We would like to thank Dominic Murphy at Bristol Regeneration Partnership for his help and support, along with Pam Vinicombe and Enitan Eboda (New Deal Office, Barton Hill) and Francine Bradshaw (volunteer community worker) for their practical help over the course of the study.

We are also grateful to the following people who read and commented on the draft report:

Adrian Coles, Building Societies Association
Shaun French, University of Bristol
Gill Hind, Financial Services Authority
Professor Jan Pahl, University of Kent
Geron Walker, Lloyds TSB Group
Mike Young, British Bankers' Association.

The study could not have been completed without the input of a range of representatives from financial services providers, not-for-profit organisations and the public sector, who agreed to be interviewed, made presentations at the select committees and commented on sections of the report.

Nor could it have been completed without the hard work of Plus Four Market Research Limited, who recruited local residents for the focus groups and select committees, and Joe McGowan who transcribed all the focus groups.

Above all, we would like to thank all the residents and workers who took part in the research for their time and commitment.

Executive summary

Despite a steady increase both in the number of households using financial services, and in the range of products they use, around 1.5 million households in Britain (7%) lack any financial products at all. A further 4.4 million (20%) are on the margins of financial services, with little more than a bank or building society account that is not much used. These households are heavily concentrated in areas of high deprivation.

As part of its strategy to combat social exclusion, the government has designated 17 'Pathfinder' neighbourhoods under its New Deal for Communities programme. This research was undertaken in one of these neighbourhoods – Barton Hill in Bristol – and was designed to identify practical ways to tackle financial exclusion there.

In its most recent document on regeneration of deprived neighbourhoods (SEU, 2001) the Social Exclusion Unit (SEU) has recommended that local residents should play a key role in developments aimed at neighbourhood regeneration. This research has adopted exactly that approach. Although other research has identified possible ways of combating financial exclusion, this study differs in that it has taken a truly 'bottom-up' approach. The methods employed in the research are, therefore, as important as the findings they have uncovered.

About the research

A participative approach was used throughout the research. Local people, who were on the margins of financial services, determined the overall direction of the research, its aims and the detail of the topics to be investigated. They were also the final arbiters on the most appropriate ways for their needs to be met.

The study began with a series of six focus groups that were designed to identify the main difficulties people experienced getting access to financial services, and the questions they would like to be put to service providers on their behalf. The 42 participants were recruited door-to-door and were all on the margins of financial services. They included men and women, people of all ages, people with disabilities and people drawn from the African Caribbean and Somali populations.

Following these discussions, 27 in-depth interviews were undertaken with a wide range of financial service providers, including commercial bodies, local and central government and the voluntary sector. The content of these interviews was determined by the questions raised in the focus groups. An audit of financial service provision was also undertaken within Barton Hill.

Finally, two 'select committees' were arranged for local people to consider the information that had been gathered, to hear at first hand from 13 of the providers who had been interviewed and to cross-examine them about the services they provide. These presenters ranged from staff from the headquarters of high street banks, the Post Office and the Association of British Credit Unions Limited, to representatives of local initiatives, such as the Portsmouth Area Regeneration Trust, a Coventry-based financial literacy project and a Norfolk micro-lending scheme for women.

Each select committee took a full day – one comprised 20 people who had taken part in the earlier focus groups, the other involved people in local organisations or the board of the Barton Hill New Deal coordinating organisation. The first of these committees identified the priorities for taking things forward; the second was convened so that people involved in developing services in Barton Hill could explore the practical issues with service providers and provide a springboard for future developments.

Local residents and local representatives were of one mind. This process was a valuable one. Local residents felt that, for the first time, they had been able to play a key role in determining how their needs for financial services might be met. The focus groups had enabled them to voice their criticisms of financial service provision and they welcomed the opportunity to hear at first hand from people designing financial services intended to meet their needs. They proved to be skilful cross-examiners in the select committee and felt a degree of optimism about future provision. Many were keen to retain an involvement in the development of local services. The study proved beyond doubt the value of giving a voice to local people.

The findings

Critics may feel that many of the findings are not especially new, and there is a good deal of truth in this – indeed it would be alarming if it were not so. But communities with high levels of financial exclusion differ in the extent and nature of the financial services to which they have ready access and hence in the needs that are paramount. If the same research process were replicated elsewhere it would identify some of the same priorities, but not all; and it would almost certainly identify problems that were not paramount in Barton Hill. These subtle differences are, however, important if appropriate services are to be developed.

Six main areas of financial service provision were identified by local residents as priorities:

- banking
- loans
- savings – but especially as a means of access to low-cost loans
- loans for micro-entrepreneurs
- financial services for Muslim Somalis
- financial information and education.

Access to insurance – and home contents insurance in particular – was also considered problematic. But it was not a high priority compared to banking, credit and savings. There was no interest in either pensions or mortgages.

Banking

Three key problems were identified in relation to personal banking. The design of bank accounts was inappropriate for people with little money who did not want to run the risk and incur the costs of inadvertently overdrawing. Although there were bank branches within Barton Hill, access was restricted by identity requirements and credit scoring. Also, people both mistrusted banks and held a very negative view of them. At the same time, they experienced difficulties managing their money without a bank account and wanted to find out if anyone was developing banking services that would better meet their needs.

At the select committee, residents were given the opportunity to discuss the new basic bank accounts offered by two high street banks – the Bank of Scotland's *Easycash* account and the National Westminster Bank's *Step* account. These were the two accounts that, at that time, exactly met the requirements of local residents. In other words, they were not subject to credit checks, required identity checks local residents could meet, offered a full range of banking services without the risk of overdrawing, but offered a small, free, buffer zone. The committee also discussed the new bill payment account that is linked to the *Easycash* account and the Post Office Universal Banking proposals.

All these developments were met with great approval. People liked the new types of account and were attracted to opening one; they especially liked the idea of banking through their local Post Office. Moreover, the new basic bank accounts were Islam-compliant. The research shows, however, that such accounts will need to be marketed sensitively.

Saving and borrowing

Although people had little money to save and were wary of borrowing, both were considered a high priority. Saving was an almost universal aspiration – for the sense of security it gives and because it can reduce dependence on high-cost credit. However, people's financial situation meant that they could only afford to save very small amounts (which they tended to do informally) and banks and building societies were not interested in such small sums, often in loose change. They wanted to find out if anyone offered a simple, but safe, savings account into which they could pay small sums of money. The Somali women wanted to know of any savings products that did not carry interest.

Borrowing was a fact of life, but people in Barton Hill had access to a very limited range of credit – moneylenders, mail order catalogues and the Social Fund.

The questions they wanted answered were: Why are people like them so often refused credit? Is their neighbourhood blacklisted? and Why do the people who *will* lend to them charge so much?

They were also interested in finding ways of breaking the link with high-cost credit so that they could begin to save. Again the Somali women wanted a non-interest-bearing source of credit.

There was widespread interest in credit unions, but little knowledge of the local one. They were also attracted to the *New Horizons* scheme where a deposit made by the Cambridge Housing Association provides tenants with access to high-interest savings accounts and linked low-cost credit. What they liked about these schemes was their local nature, the fact that they could be used to save small amounts of money, and that these savings could provide them with access to low-cost credit.

They especially liked the Cambridge 'Handy Loans' for people who had not been able to save. They were interested in the idea of 'debt buy-out', where a credit union buys out loans with door-to-door moneylenders. The Somali women raised the question of interest on savings and loans and were reassured that credit union services *could* be restructured to meet their needs even though they do not currently offer this.

The needs of micro-entrepreneurs

The study identified two distinct needs: existing micro-entrepreneurs and Somali women wanting to become self-employed.

The existing micro-entrepreneurs who took part in the study were self-employed, sole-traders who worked in the service industries. Their main needs related to access to credit for working

capital and to difficulties encountered in their dealing with banks generally. Insurance and pensions were of no interest to them at all, nor were they much interested in business advice or support. The questions they wanted asked of the banks were: What can you do for somebody like me whose needs and means are modest? and Why are you centralising all your services, as it does not appear to be for the customers' benefit? They were also interested to find out more about micro-lending schemes aimed at people like them. One of the banks interviewed said that they were prepared to look at the services they offered to self-employed people like those in Barton Hill. Locally, though, there was much greater interest in the newly launched *Street UK* – a micro-lending scheme aimed at existing micro-entrepreneurs whose needs cannot be met by the banks.

The Somali women were very interested in the possibility of becoming self-employed to break their financial dependence on the state. Indeed, some of them had already identified a business they would like to start. But they did not know how to go about it or how to raise the cash needed to start the business. Again they stressed that they would need non-interest-bearing loans.

The Norfolk women's micro-lending scheme *Full Circle*, that offers business start-up loans and support, was an attractive proposition providing that the interest on loans could be rescheduled as a charge recouped as the loan is repaid.

Financial education and information

The main needs were for education and information on banking, money management and the use of credit. People felt ill-equipped to manage their money in the early years of independent adulthood. The young people described how little they felt they knew, while the adults all said that they had learnt 'on the job', by making mistakes that were sometimes costly. Both adults and young people felt gullible in their dealings with financial service providers. They were aware that they knew very little about such things and did not trust companies, which they thought might exploit their ignorance.

It was agreed that financial literacy in schools is important, but it should not end there. The years immediately after leaving school were a crucial time for learning, as this was the time when most people need to find out about both money management and financial services generally. The adults particularly wanted to know if there was an independent source of information and advice about money matters and financial services – such as the one provided more generally by Citizens Advice Bureaux.

Two rather different projects were considered by the select committee: the *Face-to-Face with Finance* computer programme developed by the National Westminster Bank for use in schools (particularly the modules that would be most appropriate for adults), and a money management course run by Willenhall Community Advice Centre. At the time of the research there was no financial advice service of the type that residents wanted, although one was being established at Birmingham Settlement.

Perhaps surprisingly, there was as much interest in the computer programme as there was in the neighbourhood-based course. But the two were seen as complementary. The computer programme could be used by adults with their children and grandchildren who would have the necessary computer skills. The courses would be aimed at adults, with different topics being appropriate to different age groups. They were more interested in one-off sessions than a longer course. They were very interested in both courses and computer programmes being made available in a local financial advice centre.

Moving forward

All the discussions – in the focus groups, the select committees and interviews with local providers – showed that needs do not come in neat compartments. One of the clearest messages from the research was the need for a 'one-stop shop' approach to meeting unmet needs.

There were, however, some other important aspects relevant to any future development:

1. Needs would best be met by city-wide and national provision – not purely local organisations.
2. Just as important, these providers need to have a local presence in deprived areas like Barton Hill.
3. There needs to be a partnership approach between commercial companies and providers with a local presence.
4. It is important to build on existing provision and expertise and to involve local residents at all stages in the design and development of services.
5. Solutions need to be found that are sustainable.

Introduction

There has been mounting concern recently about people who have limited access to financial services and are considered financially excluded. Reflecting this interest, there has been a large body of research into the nature and causes of financial exclusion (for an overview see Kempson et al, 2000) and a wide range of developments in financial service provision that are designed to overcome it.

This report approaches the problem from a totally different standpoint – that of the people who are affected by financial exclusion personally and live in a community where many of their friends and neighbours are also excluded. It reports and analyses the range of difficulties and unmet needs for financial services expressed by local people in Barton Hill, Bristol – one of the 17 Pathfinder areas in the New Deal for Communities initiative. It documents the range of possible solutions to their needs and presents local people's assessments of the best ways to tackle the problems in their own community.

The extent and nature of financial exclusion

Despite a steady increase both in the number of households using personal financial services and in the range of products they use, around 1.5 million households in Britain (7%) lack any financial products at all. A further 4.4 million (20%) are on the margins of financial services, with little more than a bank or building society account that is often practically unused (Kempson and Whyley, 1999).

The people most likely to be excluded from, or on the margins of financial services, are those living on low incomes, especially if they are not in paid work and living on income-related benefits. The longer the head of household has been out of paid work, the more likely they are to be financially excluded. Levels of exclusion are particularly high among social tenants, lone parents, unemployed people and people from most ethnic minorities. It is higher still in areas of deprivation.

Barton Hill has above average numbers of all these groups. Incomes are low compared with the national average. Over half of residents have an income of less than £8,000 a year; 25% of households claim Income Support and 41% receive Council Tax Benefit (national figures are 19% and 23% respectively). A large proportion of households rent their home from a social landlord – 47%, compared with around 23% nationally. Levels of lone parenthood and unemployment are also well above the national average.

Finally, around 9% of residents are from ethnic minority groups, compared with 7% nationally, and just over 5% in Bristol as a whole. In particular, the area has a sizeable Somali population, most of whom are refugees.

In an area of high deprivation such as Barton Hill, around four out of 10 of the population will be on the margins of personal financial services (Kempson and Whyley, 1999). But this is not just because of the economic circumstances of the local population. Statistical modelling has shown that households living in one of the 50 most deprived local authorities had double the odds of being excluded from financial services, compared with households in similar circumstances who lived in an area of low deprivation. In other words, it is not just who you are but also where you live that determines your level of use of financial services (Kempson and Whyley, 1999).

Previous research has shown that financial exclusion is a dynamic process and many more households move in and out of financial exclusion than lack access at any one time. So, while some people have never used financial products, others have used them in the past but no longer do so. It is also a complex process. Only a small proportion of households are being denied access to all forms of personal financial service provision; and, at the other extreme, a similar proportion have made an unconstrained choice to opt out. Instead, most people who are excluded face a range of barriers. These include *price exclusion* – some financial services are too expensive; *condition exclusion* – the conditions attached to products make them inappropriate for their needs; and *marketing exclusion* – no one tries to sell them financial products. Low levels of knowledge of financial services are an additional, and very important, constraint on use (Kempson and Whyley, 1999).

Micro-entrepreneurs and start-up finance

In contrast to the personal finance market, there is less up-to-date information about the extent of financial exclusion among micro-entrepreneurs. Various studies have found that between four out of 10 and 50% of people who were seriously considering self-employment faced insurmountable obstacles raising the finance they needed (Bevan et al, 1989; Blanchflower and Oswald, 1991a, 1991b).

Those people wanting to set up small-scale enterprises who face the greatest problems raising finance from banks are those who are inexperienced and have no real track record in business, and who have limited security to back loans. Young people, women and people from ethnic minority groups are particularly disadvantaged in these ways. In addition, micro-businesses operating from premises located in high-crime areas find it difficult to gain access to insurance at prices they can afford (Kempson and Whyley, 1998a; Rogaly et al, 1998; Bank of England, 2000; Metcalf et al, 2000).

There is a good deal of evidence that people are being denied access to finance for establishing a micro-enterprise. Banks often require a detailed business plan and security before they will provide loans, and people unable to provide these are frequently refused credit. At the same time, it is clear that many micro-entrepreneurs only need small sums of credit that are too costly for high street banks to provide and, as a consequence, banks do not market their services to them (Kempson and Whyley, 1998a; Rogaly et al, 1998; Bank of England, 2000; Metcalf et al, 2000).

Levels of self-employment are relatively low in Barton Hill (5%) compared with either the national average (9%) or the average for Bristol (12%). Also, levels of registered unemployment are high (7%, compared with 4% both nationally and Bristol-wide). Moreover, the types of micro-businesses in Barton Hill are the ones most likely to face difficulty gaining access to bank finance.

Financial literacy and antipathy

Financial literacy has become an increasingly prominent issue in recent years. It is defined as "the ability to make informed judgements and to take effective decisions regarding the use and management of money" (Noctor et al, 1992, cited in DfEE, 2000a, p 4). However, although financial literacy is generally raised in the context of the financial exclusion debate, it has, in fact, been described as an inclusive, rather than an exclusive, issue (DfEE, 2000a). In other words, it has been recognised that levels of financial literacy need to be raised among most of the population, not simply those who are financially excluded or living in deprived communities. This is because developments that have taken place over the last decade mean that society now requires higher levels of financial literacy than ever before.

Yet, despite the general relevance of financial literacy to the wider population, it is likely to be a more important issue within communities such as Barton Hill for a number of reasons.

Deprived areas have a much higher concentration of people who are financially excluded and have little, if any, experience of using even fairly basic financial products such as a current account or savings account. In addition, the financial services industry often has a very limited physical presence in these areas, and financial institutions are unlikely to actively market their products and services to people living in them. As a result, people in such areas often have particularly low levels of knowledge about financial products and, more importantly, may be very suspicious of the institutions that provide them.

The fact that people living in deprived areas generally have very little money to spare means that the choices they make about financial products and services are extremely important. Similarly, the implications of making the wrong choices are likely to be much more serious. However, people living in areas like Barton Hill are very unlikely to be in a position to pay for financial advice in order to get the information they need.

Moreover, because their families, friends and neighbours are likely to be equally disengaged from financial services, they have very few sources of informal information or advice that they can draw on.

Many people living in deprived communities lack basic skills, such as literacy and numeracy. Barton Hill is no exception. This further impedes their ability to become more financially literate. Finally, deprived areas also have higher concentrations of people from minority ethnic groups – particularly recent immigrants and asylum seekers – and people who are socially excluded. These groups often face additional barriers to becoming financially literate, including language and cultural barriers, and a more serious disengagement from society in general, making them both vulnerable and difficult to reach.

Efforts to overcome financial exclusion in deprived communities have to take place within this context. Meeting the needs of households and micro-entrepreneurs that are currently excluded is not necessarily an insurmountable problem. Although most products fail to meet the design and delivery needs of low-income households, it would not require major changes to make them more appropriate. Indeed, many financial service providers are developing new products and new delivery mechanisms that are intended to fill this gap. At the same time, there are significant developments, involving the Post Office and not-for-profit organisations such as credit unions and micro-lending schemes, which are designed to combat financial exclusion and act as a gateway to mainstream financial services.

Yet it is highly likely that appropriately designed products and delivery mechanisms alone will be insufficient to encourage take-up. Many people who currently make little or no use of financial services also have very low levels of knowledge and almost no experience to draw on when deciding which products to acquire. This makes them especially vulnerable to misselling as well as encouraging self-exclusion. There is also a widespread mistrust of financial service providers and a belief that financial services are not for the poor. Again, there are good examples of schemes designed to overcome these problems that have been developed both by financial service companies and by not-for-profit organisations.

The policy context

There is widespread commitment to finding suitable ways of increasing access to financial services: within government, private companies in the financial services sector and voluntary organisations. This has, to a large extent, been stimulated by the Social Exclusion Unit (SEU) report, *Bringing Britain together* (SEU, 1998), and two follow-up Policy Action Teams (PATs) that were led by the Treasury. PAT 14 examined the scope for widening access to personal financial services for people living in poor neighbourhoods; PAT 3 investigated ways of assisting successful micro-business start-ups in poor neighbourhoods (HM Treasury, 1999a, 1999b).

Parallel, and linked to these developments, the government has announced the New Deal for Communities initiative (DETR, 1998). This aims to tackle multiple deprivation in the most deprived areas of England and Wales (there are parallel developments in Scotland). The first phase of this initiative is targeted on 17 Pathfinder areas, selected on the basis of the 1998 DETR Index of Local Deprivation. The experiences of these 17 areas will inform the extension of New Deal for Communities nationally. Barton Hill in Bristol was one of the Pathfinder areas, and included within its application for Treasury funds a proposal to develop ways of combating financial exclusion.

About Barton Hill

Barton Hill is a multicultural inner-city area, with a population of just under 6,000, that is located on the southern edge of the most deprived ward in Bristol – Lawrence Hill. It was largely redeveloped following slum clearance in the 1950s, when a considerable proportion of the existing population was dispersed to new council estates that are themselves among the most deprived areas of the city. Indeed, Barton Hill is one of a number of pockets of deprivation, left behind in Bristol's economic boom.

Geographically it is quite isolated. Construction in the 1970s of two main trunk roads and the M32 served to disconnect Barton Hill still further from the rest of the city. Despite being geographically close to the city centre, local people consistently cite poor transport links as one of the problems they face. Apart from buses to the city centre, access to other parts of Bristol is time consuming and expensive. It is also necessary to go into the city centre first to get to many other destinations, which can create difficulties for people with mobility problems and mothers with pushchairs.

Currently, 44% of the population live in housing rented from the local authority, most of them in high-rise flats. These flats are unpopular, and so they tend to be used to house people in emergencies. Consequently, there are large and growing populations of young single parents and Somali refugees. In fact, there is a 20% turnover rate in local authority tenants living in the core area of high rise and tenement buildings within Barton Hill, so that each year at least 460 people will move out of the area and a similar number move in. This level of turnover is, however, not unusual for areas of high deprivation. The remainder of the population lives mainly in private rented or owner-occupied housing, much of which is in need of refurbishment (New Deal for Communities Bristol, 1999).

Map showing Barton Hill and the New Deal for Communities area

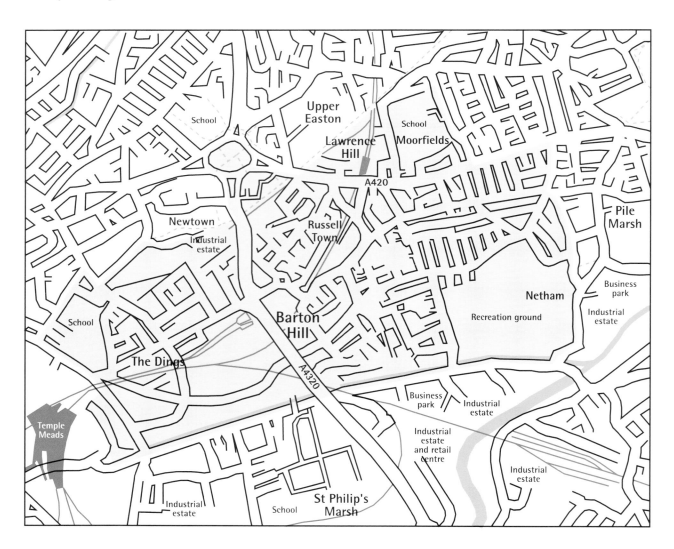

Levels of economic inactivity are high and, as a result, incomes are low compared with the national average. Altogether 35% of all people of working age are not economically active and, although the area includes five commercial/ industrial zones, over half of local businesses did not employ anyone from the local area. As mentioned earlier, more than half of residents have an income of less than £8,000 a year; 25% of households claim Income Support and a further 12% receive Jobseekers' Allowance (New Deal for Communities Bristol, 1999).

Nearly four out of 10 (37%) adults have no academic qualifications – twice the national average. Levels of literacy and numeracy problems are also high – 17% of the adult population have low literacy skills and 22% have low skills in numeracy – although no higher than the national average, according to Basic Skills Agency data (New Deal for Communities Bristol, 1999).

Crime rates in Barton Hill are high and increasing, with a particularly sharp rise in domestic burglaries (a 30% increase in six years) (New Deal for Communities Bristol, 1999). The need for home contents insurance will therefore be high, as will the premiums charged by insurance companies.

2

About the research

A large body of research has measured the extent of financial exclusion, described both its nature and causes and looked for possible solutions (see Kempson et al, 2000, for an overview). This study builds on that solid base, and has adopted a participatory approach to allow people who are actually experiencing financial exclusion to evolve practical solutions to the problems as they, themselves, see them. In its most recent document on regeneration of deprived neighbourhoods (SEU, 2001) the SEU has recommended that local residents should play a key role in developments aimed at neighbourhood regeneration. This research has adopted exactly that approach.

As a consequence, the methods employed in the research are of as much interest as the findings they have uncovered. At the end of the study there was widespread agreement that the process had been a success. People whose voices are rarely heard felt that they had played a key role in identifying, not only their most pressing needs for financial services, but also the best ways of meeting those needs. And, importantly, it started the process of breaking down the barriers between financial service providers and people who, currently, have little to do with them. In addition, financial service providers felt that they had gained valuable insights into how to extend and improve the products and services that they had designed specifically to combat financial exclusion.

The research was conducted within a neighbourhood of Bristol selected by the government to be used as a test-bed for 'joined-up solutions' to the multifaceted problems of social exclusion. Along with 16 other neighbourhoods in England and Wales, Barton Hill was designated a Pathfinder area in the New Deal for

Communities programme. Solutions identified by local residents will be fed into the 10-year plan for neighbourhood renewal in Barton Hill, which will, in part, be financed by the Treasury. National financial service providers were keen to work with Bristol-based organisations to evolve joint initiatives to overcome financial exclusion.

Critics may feel that many of the findings are not especially new. And there is a good deal of truth in this – indeed it would be alarming if that were not so. But communities with high levels of financial exclusion differ in the extent and nature of the financial services to which they have ready access and, hence, in the needs that are paramount. If the same research process were replicated elsewhere it would identify some of the same priorities but not all; and it would almost certainly identify problems that were not paramount in Barton Hill. These subtle differences are, however, important if appropriate services are to be developed.

The aim of the research

The overall aim of the research was to identify practical ways of tackling financial exclusion at a community level. Within this there were a number of specific objectives:

- to identify the priorities of local residents for increasing their access to personal financial services and appropriate ways of meeting those needs;
- to identify local needs for loans to micro-business start-ups and appropriate ways of meeting those needs;
- to explore knowledge of and attitudes to financial services, the needs for financial information and financial literacy and

appropriate ways of meeting those needs;

- to identify potential suppliers who are able and willing to meet the needs of the community and explore how this could best be achieved;
- to facilitate a dialogue between the suppliers and the local community to identify the practical initiatives that should be implemented to tackle financial exclusion in a deprived inner-city area;
- to provide a test-bed for national solutions to financial exclusion;
- to produce practical guidance for other local communities wanting to evolve plans for tackling financial exclusion.

The research process

Throughout the study a participative approach was adopted. In other words, local people who were on the margins of financial services determined both the overall direction of the research and the detailed nature of the topics to be investigated. They then reconvened to consider the information gathered on their behalf by the researchers and, through a 'select committee', to cross-examine *potential* financial service providers. They were, therefore, the final arbiters on the most appropriate ways for their needs to be met.

Initial focus groups

The research began with six focus groups that were designed to identify the main difficulties experienced by local residents in gaining access to financial services, and the questions they would like put on their behalf to service providers. The 42 group participants were recruited door-to-door and were all on the margins of financial service provision. They included both men and women, people of all ages – from 16 years to over retirement age, people with disabilities and people from the African Caribbean and Somali populations.

Two of the focus groups looked at personal financial services; one at the needs of the Somali refugee population; two at aspects of financial literacy; and one at the needs of micro-entrepreneurs. All six groups were tape-recorded and transcribed in full for detailed thematic analysis.

Personal financial services

Participants in these two groups were divided evenly into those who had no mainstream financial service products at all and those that had only an account with a bank or building society. In most instances, although they had an account, it was either a savings account or a current account that they no longer used. Only one of the 16 people was in work; the remainder were unemployed, lone parents caring for children, retired or unable to work through disability.

Both of these groups largely focused on the problems they faced with regard to basic banking needs. They identified a range of practical difficulties relating to getting and using bank accounts, as well as the problems of managing a cash budget. Above all, they voiced a strong distrust of banks. The questions they wanted put to banks on their behalf related to problems of gaining access to accounts and to the charges associated with banking.

Credit was the next most pressing need. Again it was access issues that concerned them most. They had access to a very limited range of credit – moneylenders, mail order catalogues and the Social Fund. If they needed cash loans (and most repeatedly needed small sums to make ends meet) they either borrowed from family or friends or, more commonly, borrowed from door-to-door moneylenders. The questions they wanted answered were:

- Why are people like them are so often refused credit?
- Is their neighbourhood blacklisted?
- Why do the people who *will* lend to them charge so much?

Saving was an almost universal aspiration – for the sense of security it gives and because it can reduce the dependence on high-cost credit. However, people's financial situation meant that they could only afford to save very small amounts, and banks and building societies were not interested in such small sums, often in loose change. They wanted to find out if anyone offered a simple, but safe, savings account into which they could pay small sums of money.

Insurance provision – and home contents insurance in particular – was also considered problematic, with many people being unable to afford to insure their possessions because premiums were very high and their incomes low. It was, however, given a lower priority than banking, credit or saving facilities, and there was little interest in pursuing questions relating to insurance. There were two main reasons for this. First, when money was short, home contents insurance was considered something of a luxury compared to other, more pressing daily needs that often had to be financed by short-term borrowing. Second, Bristol City Council provides an insure-with-rent scheme for its tenants at prices that are a good deal lower than the purely commercial market. This scheme was not considered ideal as it only offers indemnity insurance cover (second-hand replacement, rather than new-for-old) for fire and theft but not accidental damage. But it was felt to bridge the gap for people who had some money to spare for insurance but could not afford a policy in the open market.

The subject of pensions generated little discussion at all. Saving for a pension, or other long-term needs for that matter, was impossible and people's horizons were generally much more short-term. They were not at all interested in taking this topic further.

Although financial literacy was not the main focus of these two groups, the topic did arise during the course of the discussions. In particular, there was a strongly held belief that, because financial services are primarily aimed at the better-off, people on low incomes are told little about them and are kept in the dark. They wanted to find out if there was anyone who could offer simple explanations of financial services to people like them. Also, because managing on a low income is such a challenge, young people, and especially lone mothers, need a source of advice on money management. They wanted to know if such a service existed.

Somali women

The Somali women were young, with an age range of 21 to 31. They included married women, lone parents and one single woman without children. Half of them had a bank account although, in one case, this was a savings account. The remainder did not use any mainstream financial services.

Their discussion covered very similar ground to the previous two groups and identified

remarkably similar issues. The main difference, however, lay in their concern for financial services that met the teaching of Islam, which prohibits the receipt or payment of interest. This applied across the board – including basic banking and insurance (which was always considered unacceptable – or 'haram' – as one is insuring against acts of God), as well as the more obvious cases of credit and saving. They were, therefore, particularly interested to find out whether existing financial service providers could meet their needs or if there were any examples of specialist Islamic financial services. They had their own rotating savings and loans scheme, but felt the need for something that was rather larger and could offer business start-up finance as well as non-interest-bearing personal credit.

Financial literacy

Two further groups were recruited specifically to consider aspects of financial literacy.

One of these was a group of eight young people, aged 16-17, who had recently left school. Five of them were in full-time work, two were unemployed and one was working part-time while studying at a local further education college. All but two had a bank account. Those in work had opened a current account because their employer required them to have one for their wages to be paid into. The two unemployed young men both expected to open a current account when they found a job. Compared with the other focus group participants, these young people were more disaffected generally and found it difficult to articulate their views. For much of the time they seemed to be totally uninterested in the topic of financial services, but discussion at the end of the session showed that this was far from the truth. All but one person said that the discussion was much more interesting than they had expected and they wished it had been covered while they were at school.

As with the previous groups, much of the young people's discussion related to basic banking. During the course of this it became clear how little they knew about the services banks offered – not even the facilities available with different types of account. Those who had recently opened accounts had simply gone into the nearest bank branch and been given no choice about the type of account they could open. All had one of the basic card-based accounts aimed at young people, where all transactions have to be authorised to prevent the account being overdrawn. This would not be unusual for young people of their age. More unusually, they had almost no understanding of different types of bank accounts or of the services banks offer. This is entirely consistent with other recent research (Loumidis and Middleton, 2000).

They drew no distinction between current accounts and savings accounts and, as a consequence, wanted the same questions raised about both:

- How do I find out the interest rate?
- How much money do I need to keep in the account?
- What do banks do with my money and is it safe?
- What happens to my money if the company 'goes under'?

Beyond asking their parents these questions or putting them to someone in a bank (they did not know who), they had little idea how they would get the answers they needed.

Knowledge of credit was almost non-existent. They had heard of credit cards, mortgages and mail order catalogues, but most said that they would borrow from family or friends if they needed money. There was considerable confusion about whether people of their age could use commercial credit. Only one believed (correctly) that it was not available to people aged under 18; the rest thought that they would probably not get credit because of their low incomes and where they lived. Several had applied and been turned down, but did not know why. They had no knowledge at all about the costs of credit or the consequences if repayments were missed, nor did they have any idea how to find out, beyond asking their parents or, again, going to a bank. The main question they wanted answering was, however: Is borrowing a good idea?

Several people in the group had experience of motor insurance, although they were aware that a much wider range of policies was available to people who could afford them. Extrapolating from their experience to date they thought that access would not be difficult and the only question they wanted addressed was how best to find the cheapest policy. They said they would use the Yellow Pages to identify companies and ring around until they got the lowest quote.

They all admitted to having very poor money management skills and regularly ran out of money, even though they lived at home and had few outgoings. They all anticipated getting into financial difficulties if they moved into a place of their own and this stimulated the most lively section of the group discussion. They expected to have to learn from their mistakes and remarked that school should have prepared them better for the realities of managing their own money. Some had taken an optional business studies course at school that had covered money management, but admitted that they had not paid any attention because it seemed irrelevant at the time. Consequently, they were no more knowledgeable than the rest. They all regretted not having paid more attention at school but said it was 'boring' and they felt disaffected with teachers and school generally.

They also said they felt 'gullible' in their dealings with financial institutions and wanted ongoing information and advice that was relevant to their circumstances. They felt schools should concentrate on savings because "that is the most interesting topic" and, again, 'savings' was taken to include banking more generally. But it was suggested that these sessions should not be run by teachers, but by someone from outside the school that they could relate to. They wanted to learn about the basics of money management just before they left school, but did not want to know about borrowing until they were in work.

The second financial literacy group was of eight adults, aged over 18, who were recruited because they had taken out or considered taking out a financial product in the past year. Six of the eight had a bank account, but only three of them currently had other financial products, including one man who was a founder member of the local credit union. The remaining two people were also members of the local credit union, but used no other financial services.

For the most part, the products they had considered in the past year were loans – either from a moneylender or, in three cases, from a credit union. One woman had looked for cheaper home contents insurance when her current policy came up for renewal and one of the men had considered a life insurance policy. Only one person was in work and she had a part-time job.

The others were unemployed, retired, lone parents or partnered mothers looking after children full-time.

As with the young people, their discussion focused on banking and advice on money management and financial service provision. They wanted to find out why people face difficulties opening accounts and about the charges made by banks and the interest paid by them. This mirrors the concerns of the groups that were convened to discuss personal financial services. They also expressed a deep distrust of banks believing that they were "not for ordinary working people".

Their experiences with regard to money management had borne out the fears of the teenagers: they had learnt the hard way. Just about all of them had got into financial difficulties during the early years of independent adulthood and felt that school had not prepared them in any way for managing a household budget. They wanted to know whether there was any prospect of things improving for their children or grandchildren.

They all used credit from time to time, but only one unemployed man had credit cards that he had acquired when he had been in work. The remainder had used mail order catalogues, the credit union and door-to-door moneylenders when they needed to borrow. They knew almost nothing about the interest rates charged by different lenders – not even the ones they had used personally. Nor did they know anything about the terms and conditions of different credit sources. As in previous groups, they wanted to know why their neighbourhood was blacklisted for credit. They also wanted to know why doorstep moneylenders target low-income areas such as Barton Hill and charge people who cannot afford it such high rates of interest, and also whether the local credit union could take over much of the business currently done by doorstep lenders. They had two suggestions to make: credit unions might buy out people's loans or they could encourage people to save part of the money borrowed from moneylenders so that they would qualify for credit union loans in the future.

Taking out mortgages or pensions was considered "frightening" because it was thought to be all too easy to be misled and sales staff were not to be trusted. Neither of these products was really considered to be appropriate for the "working classes". The reduction in home-collected insurance was a source of regret – largely because people felt they could trust the agents who had, previously, visited their neighbourhood. They felt confused about the range and number of products on offer and ill-equipped to decide between them. There was widespread concern about the small print and products being poor value for money.

This group particularly wanted to know if there was a source of independent, face-to-face information and advice about money matters and financial services – similar to the one provided more generally by Citizens Advice Bureaux.

Micro-entrepreneurs

This group comprised people who were trading as self-employed. All of the participants were sole traders in the services sector who had a very low turnover. They were generally more integrated with financial services than the other five groups and had bank accounts and wider experience of credit facilities.

Their main needs related to access to credit for working capital and to difficulties encountered in their dealing with banks generally. Insurance and pensions were of no interest to them at all.

The questions they wanted asked of the banks were:

* What can you do for somebody like me whose needs and means are modest?
* Why are you centralising all your services, as it does not appear to be for the customers' benefit?

They were also interested to find out more about micro-lending schemes targeted at people like them.

Interviews with service providers

A checklist was prepared of the questions raised by the six groups. This was structured around five key areas:

* personal banking
* personal credit
* savings
* financial literacy
* loans for micro-entrepreneurs.

Interviews were then held with a total of 27 representatives of service providers who were asked for their responses to the questions raised by the focus groups and also about what services they had, or were planned, to overcome the difficulties that people in Barton Hill had raised.

The people interviewed included representatives of:

*   the Association of British Credit Unions Limited (ABCUL);
*   the Basic Skills Agency;
*   the British Bankers' Association;
*   the Campaign for Community Banking Services;
*   the DfEE secretariat for the Adult Financial Literacy Advisory Group;
*   the Financial Services Authority;
*   Post Office Counters Limited;
*   a leading credit reference agency;
*   four high-street banks;
*   four organisations involved in the delivery of financial education and training;
*   three community-based initiatives designed to combat financial exclusion;
*   three micro-lending schemes (including one already covering Barton Hill);
*   two credit unions (including one already covering Barton Hill, and one regarding financial education);
*   three Bristol-based organisations that could provide an infrastructure to build on.

All interviews were tape-recorded and transcribed for detailed analysis.

Audit of local financial service provision within Barton Hill

An audit of financial service provision within Barton Hill showed that provision is poor, but better than in some other deprived areas. Two banks have a presence in or near Barton Hill. There are two bank branches just on the boundary of the neighbourhood, and one of the banks has another branch just outside the boundary. All three branches are located on the same stretch of road, which is one of two main areas for shopping in Barton Hill. However, these branches are not accessible to everyone who lives in Barton Hill. Moreover, the road has one of the highest rates of traffic accidents in the city.

Most people living in Barton Hill do have easy access to a Post Office. Three Post Offices serve the area and there are several others just outside the boundary; consequently most people have less than half a mile walk to their nearest one. There are also two PayPoint outlets within Barton Hill (outlets for the payment of household bills at local shops and petrol stations), one of which stays open until 10pm.

As local crime rates are high, insurance is expensive. Bristol City Council therefore runs an insure-with-rent scheme offering its tenants low-cost home contents insurance with the premium being paid in instalments with their rent.

Weekly-collected credit companies are very active in Barton Hill and there is also evidence of illegal moneylenders. There is a newly formed credit union – Money-go-Round – that covers the inner-city area of Bristol and has a weekly collection point in Barton Hill. Bristol Enterprise Development Fund offers loans to micro- and small businesses that are located in deprived parts of the city and cannot gain access to bank finance. And two micro-lenders provide loans and assistance to young people who want to become self-employed – the Prince's Trust and the Young Entrepreneurs' Development Fund.

Barton Hill Settlement – an umbrella community-based organisation – has a long-standing record of community development in the area. In particular, it has developed innovative approaches to literacy that could form the basis for financial literacy and financial information initiatives.

Two select committees

When the interviews and local audit of financial service provision were complete, two 'select committees' were arranged to allow local residents to consider the information that had been gathered and identify a plan for future developments in Barton Hill.

One committee was drawn primarily from the people who had attended the focus groups. At the end of the focus groups, participants were asked if they would like to take part in later stages of the study when we considered the answers to the questions they had raised. Just about everyone said that they were interested. In the event, not everyone was invited back. We did not, for example, include the micro-entrepreneurs as they had such different needs to other participants. In addition, some people were not free on the day and so could not attend. A total of 20 people actually participated, including three men recruited specifically for the select committee to redress the gender imbalance created by the men who could not make it on the day.

The select committee with local residents lasted for a full day and was divided into three sessions that covered, in turn, personal banking, savings and loans and financial literacy. The sessions were separated by breaks for coffee/tea or lunch. Further details of the topics covered are given in Box 1.

Each session began with the facilitator reminding committee members of the questions and issues that had arisen out of the focus groups. They were told the outcomes of the interviews that we had carried out and, in particular, the answers we had obtained to the questions they wanted us to ask on their behalf. Next they were told which financial service providers we had invited to make presentations to them and why these people had been chosen. Following this there was a brief discussion of the questions they might want to raise with the presenters. This 'preparation' typically lasted for around half an hour for each session.

The financial service providers were then invited to speak, in turn, for around 10-15 minutes each, with a similar length of time for questions and discussion. The session then finished with an overall discussion of the topic by the select committee members to form a view of the initiatives they had heard about and decide which ones, if any, they thought would be appropriate to the needs of people like them living in Barton Hill. The financial service providers were not present during these discussions.

By structuring the sessions in this way the strain on participants was minimised, although all said that they felt tired by the end of the day. None had ever taken part in a day-long meeting or seminar before. Indeed they said they had done nothing remotely like it since leaving school. Nevertheless, they found the day interesting and many said they would like to be involved in developing services within Barton Hill.

The second select committee had not been planned from the outset. However, it became apparent during the research that it would be valuable to hold a parallel committee involving people employed in local organisations and local resident members of the board of the Barton Hill New Deal coordinating body – Community at Heart. It was thought that this would strengthen

Box 1: Barton Hill Select Committee for Local Residents, September 2000

	Topic	Presentations
9.30–10.00am	Introduction and briefing	
10.00–10.45am	Financial education and training	• *Face-to-Face with Finance* programme, NatWest Bank • Money management training course, Willenhall • Community Advice Centre
10.45–11.15am	*Coffee and feedback*	
11.15am–1.00pm	Banking services	• *Step* account, NatWest Bank • *Easycash* and *Bill Payment* accounts, Bank of Scotland • *Universal Banking Service*, Post Office Counters Ltd
1.00–1.30pm	*Lunch and feedback*	
1.30–2.30pm	Saving and borrowing	• Money-go-Round Credit Union, Bristol • Portsmouth Area Regeneration Trust • *New Horizons* savings and loans scheme, Cambridge • Housing Association
2.30–3.00pm	*Tea and feedback*	

Box 2: Barton Hill Select Committee for Local Workers and Representatives, September 2000

	Topic	Presentations
9.30–10.15am	Introduction and briefing	
10.15–11.00am	Micro-lending	• Bristol Enterprise Development Fund • Full Circle, Women's Enterprise, Employment and Training Unit • Street (UK)
11.00–11.30am	*Coffee and feedback*	
11.30am–12.30pm	Saving and borrowing	• Association of British Credit Unions Limited • Portsmouth Area Regeneration Trust • *New Horizons* saving and loan scheme, Cambridge • Housing Association
12.30–1.00pm	*Lunch and feedback*	
1.00–2.00pm	Financial education and training	• *Face-to-Face with Finance* programme, NatWest Bank • Money management training course, Willenhall • Community Advice Centre
2.00–4.00pm	Moving forward: what role can banks play?	• Discussion with headquarters' representatives of the two clearing banks with branches in Barton Hill
4.00–4.30pm	*Tea and summing up*	

the research but, more particularly, would pave the way to implementing the results of the research with local residents. This select committee addressed four key issues: savings and loans; finance for micro-entrepreneurs; financial literacy; and working with banks to develop community-based finance covering Bristol (Box 2). The facilitator of the residents' select committee joined the second committee for this final session, to relay the views of local residents. Otherwise, the format was broadly similar to the one adopted for the local residents' select committee.

Both select committees were tape-recorded and detailed notes prepared from the tapes for analysis.

This report

The remainder of this report brings together the findings from the various stages of the study as they relate to the key areas identified by the focus groups at the outset of the research. Subsequent chapters, therefore, deal in turn with personal banking, saving and borrowing, financial

education and information, and the needs of micro-businesses.

In terms of meeting local needs, two things became clear during the course of the research. First, that there is a need for portable solutions to the aspects of financial exclusion identified above. High levels of population turnover mean that purely local solutions will always be inadequate as a long-term solution for people who spend a relatively brief period of their lives in Barton Hill, or other similar communities. Second, that people's unmet needs for financial services do not come in neat compartments. Consequently, financial services need to be delivered locally in a 'joined-up' fashion. In practical terms this means national and city-wide organisations working together to provide wide-ranging community finance initiatives through local outlets in deprived communities. These ideas are expanded in the final chapter.

3

Personal banking services

Nationally, the proportion of households lacking a bank or building society account of any type is between 6% and 9% (Kempson and Whyley, 1998b; Office of Fair Trading, 1999). Barton Hill residents share many of the characteristics associated with not having an account. Non-account holding is concentrated among people on low incomes and those on Income Support in particular. It is especially high for unemployed people and lone parents. Levels of account holding are low among ethnic minority groups. Social tenants are also much more likely to lack an account than owner-occupiers (Kempson and Whyley, 1998b). As noted in Chapter 1, Barton Hill has above average numbers among all these groups.

Local people highlighted a number of key issues in relation to personal banking, which can be broadly categorised as:

- inappropriate design of bank accounts;
- lack of access to banking services;
- negative views and mistrust of banks and other financial institutions.

There is a considerable degree of overlap between these three areas so that, in combination, they create a formidable barrier to accessing and using banking services.

Inappropriate design of bank accounts

It is widely acknowledged that the great majority of current accounts are inappropriate to the budgeting needs of people living on low incomes, and this was reaffirmed by the residents of Barton Hill. The main difficulties with such accounts are their lack of transparency, the fact that it is possible to overdraw, and the charges imposed

for overdrawing (see, for example, National Consumer Council, 1997; Kempson and Whyley, 1999; Office of Fair Trading, 1999). Local people were also concerned about the charges levied by banks for withdrawing money from cash machines. Put another way, operating a cash budget allows people to keep much tighter control over their finances than is possible with most bank accounts.

Closely linked to this was the overwhelming belief that a bank account was simply *irrelevant* for people living on a low income, and in particular, on state benefits. Consequently, many people said that they would only think about opening an account if they became employed. In addition, a number of people regarded a bank account more as a vehicle for saving than a tool for day-to-day money management. As they were living on low incomes and not able to save any money, they saw no value in having or using a bank account.

Lack of transparency

Money transactions conducted through a current account (such as purchases made with a debit card, direct debits and standing orders) cause the greatest problems with regard to transparency. As previous research has noted, people living on a low income want to be able to work out, at any given time, which transactions have already been completed, which payments remain outstanding, and exactly how much money they have available (Kempson and Whyley, 1999). In other words, they want 'real-time' information about their account.

These concerns were reflected by the Barton Hill residents. While some focus group participants recognised the value of direct debits as a convenient and potentially cheaper means of paying bills, most regarded them as risky and potentially costly. The greatest fear was that money might be debited from an account on the 'wrong day' (that is, when there was not enough money in the account to cover it) leaving the account-holder with hefty charges for overdrawing. This had in fact happened to a number of participants in the past, prompting them to suspend use of the account:

> "... a direct debit went in two days before it should have ... and they charge me £27.50 to turn down £9 – it was £9 for my water bill and they charged me £27.50 to refuse it."

The length of the banks' clearing cycle added to concerns about transparency. One woman, for instance, questioned the length of time it took for her husband's wage cheque to clear every month:

> "That's another thing, three clear days to cash a cheque – that's no good to a man who is paid once a month, and he's got to wait almost a week again before he can get a wage out, that's ridiculous."

As they did not have an overdraft facility, this couple sometimes struggled to make ends meet in the days before the husband's wage cheque had cleared.

Overdrawing

People's views about overdrafts were rather contradictory. Some focus group participants identified a need for a small overdraft facility (in the range of £20 to £50) to 'tide them over' until they received their next wages or benefit payment, or for use in an emergency. Others did not want any overdraft facility at all.

A number of people talked about problems they had experienced in the past with overdraft facilities. For example, one man told how his overdraft limit had been reduced by the bank because he had used it too much. Despite this, he had continued to receive credit card marketing information from the bank, which he felt was nonsensical:

> "They wanted me to have a credit card, Visa, and you can have up to £1,000 on this Visa card but they're not even allowing me to go over into the buffer zone ... so it's a bit stupid."

Charges

A pervasive view among focus group participants was that banks charged "for everything", making them unaffordable for people on low incomes. One person, for example, thought that she would be charged for transferring her account to another bank. Negative media coverage about banks around the time of the focus groups, and about cash machine charges in particular, may well have added fuel to these beliefs.

Fear of charges and the risk of getting into debt underpinned people's concerns about overdrafts. Many people felt, therefore, that bank accounts were not appropriate for them because of the danger of incurring considerable charges if they should inadvertently overdraw the account.

Somali people face a particular problem with regard to overdrafts because, as Muslims, they are not allowed to use financial products that are interest-bearing or interest-earning. One young Somali woman had, for this reason, stopped using her bank account altogether when she unintentionally became overdrawn. She is currently using her sister's account instead.

With regard to charges for using cash machines, people felt strongly that it was unfair to have to pay to get your own money out, especially if you were living on a low income. As one woman put it:

> "... in other words, the bank is getting richer and I'm getting poorer. And I'm already poor."

Lack of access to banking services

Lack of access to banking services has three main dimensions for the people of Barton Hill. First, many lack the forms of identification that have traditionally been required by banks to open an account, such as a passport or driving licence. (Under current money laundering legislation, all banks, building societies and other financial services providers have to obtain proof of identity and address from consumers. Most prefer passports and driving licences because they are issued by an official authority, cannot be easily forged and include a photograph.) This is a particular issue for Somali people living in the area, most of whom are refugees:

> "Say, if you've only been in the country for one year now and they ask you, 'What was your last address and where did you live?'.... When you've only lived here for a certain time, you know, for about a year or so, you don't have a passport, you don't have any of the identifications. They should be happy if you give them your travel documents, or something like that, because that's all you've got – you don't have a driving licence, nothing."

The second dimension is geographical. As mentioned in Chapter 2, two banks have a presence in or near Barton Hill – one with two branches, the other with one branch. However, all three bank branches are located on the same busy stretch of road, which is not easily accessible to people living in the Dings neighbourhood of Barton Hill. In addition, the road is a notorious accident 'black spot', with one of the highest rates of road traffic accidents in the city. People also voiced concerns about possible bank branch closures in the area, which could leave them without a bank at all. People who have an account somewhere other than the two local banks face a fairly lengthy journey to get to their nearest branch; the cost of travelling by public transport is also high.

Finally, focus group participants frequently spoke about being unable to access bank accounts (and other financial services) because of their address – that is, they believed parts of Barton Hill had been 'blacklisted' by banks and other financial institutions. Consequently, several of them saw little point in even trying to apply for a bank account:

> "Because the banks go by postcodes ... they look at your postcode and say, 'Oh, Barton Hill', they'll say, 'No, that is blacklisted, we can't give you anything like that'."

In addition, one woman who had tried to open an account believed she was turned down because of bad debts incurred by previous occupants:

> "I managed to get enough ID and then they turned me down because of my

address, because the address is blacklisted from the previous people that lived there ... I didn't want anything special, it was just simply for wages to be paid in; I didn't want an overdraft or anything like that, but they still wouldn't even let me have anything like that."

In fact, 'blacklisting by address', whether because of previous occupants or based on a postcode, seems unlikely. It is more likely that people have been refused bank accounts (or other financial services) because of their constrained financial and economic circumstances. The concentration of people living under such circumstances, on housing estates or in particular areas, merely reinforces the misperception that certain neighbourhoods are being 'redlined' by financial services providers. These issues are explored further in Chapter 4.

Views of banks

Other concerns notwithstanding, possibly the greatest barrier to accessing banking services was people's mistrust of banks and other financial institutions. First, people felt very strongly that banks did not understand, and indeed were not interested in, the needs of people living on low incomes:

> "They have got to realise what it's like at the bottom – it's really, really hard. So if they want us to know about banks, and know what is going to be good for us and everyone else, then they've got to start from the bottom and try their hardest to get through to the people."

This perceived lack of understanding was echoed by a number of Somali people, and by the participants in the micro-business focus group. Similarly, several people spoke of feeling embarrassed and belittled when they tried to deal with bank staff:

> "It just annoys me, because the people on the desk they're just so snotty, and they look down on you."

Second, banks were considered to be 'a rip-off', only interested in making as much money as possible from their customers. Consequently, they were seen as being quick to offer loans but slow to offer a good transactional banking service.

Some of these views are undoubtedly based on people's own experience of using banks. But, given the high level of disengagement from financial services among local people, it seems likely that this is combined with a firmly entrenched 'received wisdom' that banks simply 'aren't for them'. Overcoming these psychological barriers will be vital in promoting financial inclusion.

Managing without a bank account

Although local people identified problems of getting and using a bank account, they also acknowledged some of the difficulties of managing *without* a bank account.

As discussed above, many people were reluctant to use direct debits. Even so, they recognised the advantages of direct debits as a convenient and potentially cheaper means of paying bills. Moreover, there were costs and disadvantages associated with the forms of bill payment that they used instead. One woman, for example, had her telephone disconnected because of a delay in transmitting her payment from a PayPoint outlet to the telephone company:

> "... I said to them that I have paid my bill at a certain place, at the PayPoint and paid the money, zipped the card through the machine, 'phoned them up and gave them the serial number off the receipt and they said, no, they hadn't received it yet. The next day I 'phoned them up, give them the receipt number – 'oh, I haven't received it yet'. Three days later they received it and in the meantime my 'phone is cut off and I had to pay another £35 to get it back on."

Accepting a job could be more difficult without a bank account, as employers increasingly require workers to have wages paid by automatic transfer. Indeed, previous research indicates that financially excluded households perceive this as a barrier to employment (Burrows, 1999; Kempson and Whyley, 1999; Speak and Graham, 2000). Finally, a number of people talked about the difficulties of dealing with cheques issued to them. While some were happy to use commercial cheque cashing

outlets, others could not even do this because they lacked the types of identification required.

Although it was not raised in the focus groups, the government announced on 24 May 1999 its intention to pay all pensions and state benefits directly into a bank or building society account from 2003. From that date, therefore, everyone receiving these payments will need to have an account.

Meeting the needs for personal banking services

Over the past few years, the banking sector has begun to address many of the difficulties concerning access to services and product design identified by the residents of Barton Hill. A number of initiatives intended to offer solutions to these problems are examined below.

Design of bank accounts

Many of the issues and concerns raised by the people of Barton Hill are currently being addressed by the banking industry. Earlier research provided a useful 'blueprint' for the type of bank account that people living on low incomes would ideally like to use (Kempson and Whyley, 1999). This idea of a basic, no-frills account was taken forward by PAT 14, established by the SEU to look specifically at access to financial services.

The key features of a 'basic' bank account include access to cash through automatic teller machines, and use of a Solo/Electron debit card (where the cardholder's account is checked before any transaction is approved). A transaction only takes place, therefore, if there is sufficient cash in the cardholder's account to cover it. The key benefit of this type of account is that it allows very close control over all monies, matching the type of control possible when dealing with cash. Also, a chequebook is not provided with such accounts, nor can the account become overdrawn. Consequently it does not have to be credit scored. Some accounts allow all the money in the account to be withdrawn – down to the last penny if required – by providing a 'buffer zone', which is effectively an interest and charge-free overdraft facility of about £10.

Bank of Scotland *Easycash* and *Bill Payment* accounts

Easycash account

- Cash card with 'real-time' debit facility.
- No overdraft facility, but small 'buffer zone' to allow people to withdraw last penny in the account.
- No cheque book.
- No charges for using ATMs or counter withdrawals.
- No charges for direct debits or standing orders.

Bill Payment account

- A linked *Bill Payment* account is available to Bank of Scotland current account holders, including *Easycash* account holders, for people who want to spread the cost of their household bills.
- A set amount is paid from the current account into the *Bill Payment* account either weekly or monthly. All bill payments are then made directly to the listed companies.
- Flat fee of £20 to set up the *Bill Payment* account; one standing order charge of 50p levied each payment cycle, no matter how many bills are paid.
- Overdraft facility equivalent to one week's or one month's bills, 13% interest charged on this.

Encouragingly, it appears that banks and building societies have taken up the challenge of developing these types of accounts. The British Bankers' Association and Committee of Scottish Clearing Bankers recently announced that all the main banks have new accounts that fit these requirements (see www.bba.org.uk/consumers).

The Building Societies Association has stated that many of its members are doing the same. Some banks (for example the Bank of Scotland) have gone one step further and designed a bill payment facility available to all current account holders, including the basic bank account, for people who want to spread the cost of their household bills over the year.

On the whole, the local people who took part in the select committee were receptive to the new types of bank accounts presented to them. However, most people experessed considerable

NatWest *Step* account

The *Step* account, available from October 2000, aims to provide a route into financial services. Its main features include:

- Free transactional banking.
- No opening balance needed to start the account, no minimum amount required to keep the account open, and monthly interest paid on credit balances.
- Cash card gives access to money from ATMs, NatWest branches and via retail cash-back.
- 'Real-time' debit card facility.
- No credit facilities attached to the account, and no cheque book.
- Money can be paid in using a paying-in book, through ATMs, or via direct debits and standing orders.

antipathy to the term 'basic bank account', as it conjured up images of a second-rate product accompanied by a second-rate service. This initial wariness was largely dispelled when the accounts were described in greater detail as being possible gateways to other mainstream financial services.

The key features of basic bank accounts also met with approval. People clearly valued a product that was designed to let them keep tight control over their finances – there was general agreement, therefore, that they did not want a chequebook nor an overdraft facility.

Some concerns were raised regarding the security of cash cards. In particular, people were worried about cards being stolen and used fraudulently, largely because they were under the impression that the cardholder would be liable for any costs incurred by misuse of the card. They were very surprised to be told that, in those situations, liability lies with the bank rather than the cardholder.

Several people were attracted by the idea of a linked bill-payment facility, such as that provided by the Bank of Scotland, that allowed them to pay a fixed amount either weekly or monthly to help spread the cost of bills over the year. It was notable that some said they would use a similar service if it was offered by the Post Office.

Access to banking services

Since the Money Laundering Regulations became law in 1994, all banks, building societies and other businesses providing financial services have had to put procedures in place to prevent money laundering. As a result, anyone who wishes to open an account or buy financial products has to provide proof of identity and address.

This issue has now been addressed in the Financial Services Authority's (FSA) new rules on money laundering. These will allow banks to accept as evidence of identity a letter or statement from a 'person of responsibility' who knows the applicant. Examples of such people given by the FSA include hostel managers and social workers; other examples might be district nurses and midwives. The new rules are expected to come into force by the middle of 2001.

In fact, the banking industry has already taken a number of positive steps towards addressing the issue of identification. Several banks have broadened their identification requirements to include items such as household bills and medical cards. The Bank of Scotland accepts introductions from three charities, including *The Big Issue*, whose vendors can use their *Big Issue* ID card as one form of proof, along with either a medical card or birth certificate. As vendors are often homeless or in temporary accommodation, the address of *The Big Issue* office is used as the vendor's address; vendors can then collect their bank statements from the office. Lloyds TSB has established a telephone helpline so that counter staff can check whether the proof of identity presented by a customer is acceptable. Finally, the British Bankers' Association has produced a leaflet for consumers entitled *You and proving your identity* (BBA Enterprises Limited, 1999), and, in association with energy companies, they have devised a simple letter that people with fuel pre-payment meters could be given by their supply company for use in lieu of a utility bill.

Even so, there was some indication from the focus groups that increased flexibility regarding identity requirements has not yet filtered down to branch level. One young woman related how she had been refused a bank account because she could not provide a birth certificate or driving licence. The bank would not accept a utility bill as proof of address, nor did they suggest alternative forms of identity that she might be able to provide instead.

Geographical access

It is impossible to predict the likelihood of bank branch closure in Barton Hill, although future closures cannot be ruled out. In response to the reduction of bank branch networks nationally, a number of new and innovative delivery channels are being developed and tested, many involving partnerships between the private, public and not-for-profit sectors.

While geographical access to a bank branch is difficult for some local residents (as discussed above), most have easy access to a Post Office. Starting with Alliance & Leicester Girobank, the Post Office has, over the years, been building up agency agreements with other high street banks to offer transactional services. These include the Cooperative Bank, Lloyds TSB and Barclays. Other banks seem likely to follow suit, particularly once the automation of the Post Office network has been completed (it is planned that the entire network will be automated by summer 2001; Performance and Innovation Unit, 2000).

In addition, there are proposals for a 'universal banking service', to be operated by the Post Office with support from some high street banks, and aimed predominantly at meeting the banking needs of people living in deprived communities. This will include making basic bank accounts usable at local Post Offices.

Post Office Universal Banking Service

The main aim of the Post Office's Universal Banking Service is to provide a range of bank accounts designed to meet customers' needs. Accordingly, the Post Office proposes to offer three tiers of personal banking:

1. 'Traditional' bank accounts through existing agency agreements.
2. 'Basic' bank accounts, available at all Post Office counters.
3. 'Universal' bank accounts – a stripped down version of the basic bank account, whereby the account holder can have money paid into the account, and will have a cash card enabling them to draw the money out over the counter from any Post Office, but no other facilities.

The Bank of Scotland has been piloting several projects to provide some form of banking facility in areas of Scotland that have no branch. One of these is a partnership scheme with Greater Easterhouse Development Company to set up a banking facility in Easterhouse Ideas Shop. (Two other banks – Lloyds TSB and, more recently, Barclays – have participated in experimental community banks. In contrast with the Easterhouse development, these concentrate on providing credit facilities and are described in the following chapter.) Moreover, bank accounts and other financial services could potentially be provided through organisations such as credit unions, local authorities and Registered Social Landlords; a number of these projects are currently in the pipeline.

However, for the select committee participants, delivery of banking services was simply a question of "banks versus the Post Office". And, for the most part, the Post Office came off best. A number of factors combine to explain this strength of opinion.

First, unlike the banks, the Post Office is easily accessible for almost all Barton Hill residents, regardless of the neighbourhood they live in. Second, people already use their local Post Office regularly, most often to collect state benefits but also to pay their household bills, to buy TV licence savings stamps, or to get their weekly lottery ticket. Consequently, people preferred to deal with the Post Office than banks because they knew the staff, the staff appeared to be friendlier, and the atmosphere of the Post Office was less formal than that of the bank:

> "... everything's clinical [in the bank], whereas with the post office you can go in and draw your benefits and that, and you can have a chat ... it's that sort of interacting thing with people, around in your own community. Whereas with a bank, you go in and it's just bam, bam, bam [mimes rubber stamping]."

Finally, people felt that the Post Office was easier to deal with than a bank – indeed, banks seemed to always make matters unduly complicated.

On the whole, then, people preferred the idea of banking with their local Post Office rather than dealing directly with banks. And, taken on balance, the *provider* appeared to be just as

important as the *product* in determining people's opinions about new types of banking services.

To sum up, there have been a number of positive developments aimed at increasing access to personal banking services. Greater flexibility regarding identity requirements, coupled with the development of more appropriate bank accounts, and the emergence of partnership arrangements to deliver banking services, will hopefully make it easier for people living on low incomes to open and use bank accounts that more closely meet their needs. In the longer term, greater integration into the banking system may help overcome the negative views and mistrust that are so deeply ingrained within communities such as Barton Hill.

4

Saving and borrowing

To a large extent, saving and borrowing have not been considered central to debates on financial exclusion, albeit for different reasons. Access to, and use of, savings products are perceived to be desirable rather than essential. Even so, it is generally recognised that savings provide security (actual and psychological), act as a safety-net in the face of unforeseen events and smooth the household budget during times of financial constraint.

In contrast, borrowing is often seen as something that exacerbates the problems faced by low-income households. But, while borrowing money to supplement a low income may not be desirable, it is often unavoidable – either to buy essential household items or to make ends meet (Kempson and Whyley, 1999).

The residents of Barton Hill considered access to these products to be important, despite the fact that most had little money to save, and were wary of borrowing.

Borrowing

Use of consumer credit has risen dramatically in the past two decades, as a result of rising real incomes and a rapid growth in the range of products available, combined with more aggressive marketing to a much broader customer base. Nonetheless, it is estimated that around 29% of households have no access to credit from a mainstream provider (Office of Fair Trading, 1999; Kempson and Whyley, 2000).

For the residents of Barton Hill, concerns revolved mainly around their limited choice of sources of borrowing (including perceived exclusion from mainstream lenders). Participants in one of the focus groups also raised the problem of breaking the link with door-to-door moneylenders, and this was reiterated in interviews with local community workers. The greatest problem for the Muslim Somali population was the lack of Islam-compliant products.

Limited choice of credit

Very few people in the focus groups had ever used mainstream credit. A couple of people had used credit and debit cards in the past, but stopped using them altogether when they got into financial difficulties.

Moreover, many of those who had never used mainstream credit were deterred from ever applying because of 'third party blacklisting', that is, they firmly believed they could be refused credit because of debts incurred by previous occupants:

> "It is all this red tape, and it just stems from one council house, one council flat, you could have had one person in there, say, 10 years ago, done an awful lot of wrong. So the people that have followed on, they don't know how to get their name clear; they can't afford to get their name cleared because they are living in that flat, and it has been blacklisted for the last 10 years. So you go to the bank, all they will look into is, 'Oh no, such-and-such address, sorry'."

According to industry experts, however, 'third party blacklisting' by creditors is extremely unlikely. Not only is it illegal, but, since 1993, the Data Protection Registrar has sought to prohibit the use of information about anyone other than people with the same surname living at the same address in the assessment of credit applications. In the autumn of 2001 this will be tightened still further to prohibit the use of information about anyone other than the individual applicant.

It is more probable that people have been refused credit for one of a number of reasons. First, because of their financial circumstances, people living on low incomes are unlikely to pass the credit scoring needed to gain access to most consumer credit. In addition to credit scoring, financial providers have policy rules which govern whether they lend to certain groups of people or not. Based on these rules, they might not even process an application from someone who had, say, been unemployed for a certain length of time.

There may also be a link between electoral registration and refusal. Anecdotal evidence suggests that people are reluctant to register because they (wrongly) believe that it is linked to payment of Council Tax. In the two wards covering Barton Hill, over one in five adults are not on the electoral roll. Most lenders set considerable store by electoral registration, as it can be used to confirm details such as the applicant's address. Some lenders will immediately (and legally) reject people who are not on the electoral register without conducting any further credit checks.

In combination, low levels of electoral registration in particular wards, and the concentration of people with low credit ratings living on certain housing estates or in specific areas may give the impression of 'redlining' by lenders. This view is possibly being fuelled by inadequate communication and explanation about reasons for refusal by lenders.

According to the recently revised *Guide to credit scoring* (Finance and Leasing Association, 2000), if an application for credit is refused, the lender should advise the unsuccessful applicant of the *principal reason* for refusal. This includes refusal on the grounds of an inadequate credit score, in which case the lender should also give an indication of the type of information that was included in the scorecard (Finance and Leasing Association, 2000). In practice, the quality of information provided by lenders may vary considerably.

Moreover, refused applicants may be unwilling to contact the lender, or may be unaware that they can do so. Without knowing the actual reason for refusal, 'third party blacklisting' may seem as good an explanation as any.

Sources of credit used

Excluded for the most part from mainstream sources, people in Barton Hill were faced with a limited choice of credit, much of which was high-cost. Not surprisingly, they tended to use the types of credit usually associated with life on a low income: mail order catalogues, the Social Fund Budgeting Loan scheme, friends and family, and door-to-door moneylenders. In addition, several people who participated in the study were credit union members, and the Somali women were all members of a community-based rotating savings and loan scheme.

Mail order catalogues

Mail order catalogues were used widely, both because people liked the convenience of shopping from home and also because mail order allowed them to spread the costs of everyday items interest free. However, the high mark-up on most mail order goods can equate to an APR (annual percentage rate) of 150% or above.

Social Fund Budgeting Loan scheme

Quite a number people had experience of using the Social Fund Budgeting Loan scheme; it was particularly common among younger women with children. They liked the scheme primarily because it provided interest-free loans for 'lumpy' expenditure, such as washing machines and beds. The direct deduction of loan repayments from benefits was also popular, although a number of people thought the repayment rates were too high. Other drawbacks included the upper limit placed on loan applications, and the fact that applicants often do not get the full amount they apply for (see also Whyley et al, 2000).

Borrowing from friends and family

Borrowing from friends and family was fairly common among the focus group participants; indeed, for some, it formed an ongoing part of their household budgeting.

"I borrow money a fiver here and there off my friends. Come Monday when I get my money, I feel, 'Oh my God I can't pay her back', but I have to because at least that way, if I pay them back, I can borrow it again."

As we know from earlier research, this type of reciprocal lending is common among low-income households, and among women in particular (Kempson et al, 1994).

Credit union loans

The Money-go-Round credit union covers the whole of inner-city Bristol, and has a weekly collection point in Barton Hill. Several people who took part in the study were active members of the credit union, and had taken out loans for items such as clothing and furniture.

Rotating savings and loans schemes

As a result of the religious rules prohibiting Muslims from paying or receiving interest, the Somali people living in Barton Hill are faced with even fewer options for borrowing money. Most used the Social Fund Budgeting Loan scheme for larger items, and borrowed small amounts from their friends or family to make ends meet.

In addition, all the Somali women who took part in the focus group were members of a rotating savings and loans club. These schemes are common among many minority ethnic groups, and all work in much the same way. A group of (usually) friends agree to meet regularly and save a set amount of money. At each meeting the savings are collected, and one member receives the total amount accrued. The order in which people qualify for the payment may be pre-determined at the outset, or it may be decided by drawing lots at each meeting (Kempson, 1998).

In the case of the Somalis' scheme, each member saved at least £10 a week. The club met twice a month to collect and distribute the pooled money. The money was usually distributed according to a pre-agreed order, although a member could receive money out of turn if they needed it urgently. Most people in the focus group used the money to buy clothes for their children or to pay household bills.

The obvious advantage of the scheme was that they did not pay interest on the amount received. On the downside, each member had to wait their turn to receive the lump sum payment, and it could be a struggle to find the required contribution each week:

"You still have to be able to budget your money so much, so that you can be able to pay for the group as well as being able to buy your own food, pay the bills and all that stuff."

Even though the club was certainly a valuable source of money for its members, participants wanted to be able to access larger amounts of money, preferably from a Somali-run organisation.

Licensed moneylenders

A number of people had experience of using licensed moneylenders, mostly for cash loans. As other research has noted, the very high cost of these loans (APRs typically range from between 100% for loans of £500 or more, repaid over 100 weeks, and 400-500% for a £60 loan repaid in 20 weeks; Rowlingson, 1994) is often outweighed by the fact that they are specifically designed to meet the needs of people living on low incomes. People are attracted by easy access to small sums of money, borrowed over relatively short periods of time. They like the fact that weekly repayments are collected from their home and, although people know the loans are expensive, they appreciate the total transparency of the costs involved (Kempson and Whyley, 2000).

However, several focus group participants talked about the financial difficulties created by using weekly-collected credit. One woman had taken out a 'roll-over' loan totalling £420, to pay off her existing loan and buy a computer for her son's birthday, even though she knew that she would struggle to keep up with the repayments:

"You will agree to whatever terms they say to you, as long as you get what you want at the end of it."

In addition, unreliable collection of weekly loan repayments had led several people to get into arrears:

"They'd turn up when they could be bothered to pick up your payments, and if they didn't pick the payments up then you'd spend the money. Simple as that."

Unlicensed moneylenders

Unlicensed moneylenders, or 'loan sharks', are known to be widespread across low-income communities. The focus groups in Barton Hill provided evidence of unlicensed moneylenders operating in the area and in other areas of Bristol. For example, one man told how his daughter had borrowed £20 on a Friday to tide her over the weekend, and had to repay £40 the following Monday. Given that the APR for this loan repaid over one month is over 400,000%, it is likely that the APR over three days amounts to at least several million per cent.

Breaking the link with moneylenders

A number of people in the focus groups talked about getting 'trapped' into a cycle of using moneylenders (both licensed and unlicensed), partly through lack of choice, but also because of the aggressive marketing strategies employed by some companies:

> "It's easy, though, to get into the trap with [company name] because they come banging on your door, and you've got some people that have got young kids and that, they just come round, 'Do you want vouchers?'."

Several credit union members who took part in one of the focus groups, as well as local community workers interviewed during the research, were interested in the role that credit unions could potentially play in providing cheaper alternatives to weekly-collected credit. This is explored in detail opposite.

Saving

Most people in the focus groups felt that saving was important – for security, for their children's future and, among the Somali people, to send money back to relatives in Somalia. Saving for old age was generally considered less important, probably because the majority of people felt that they were either too young or too poor to even consider contributing to a pension.

Although they considered it to be important, focus group participants were able to save little, if anything, from their income. As we might expect, issues of affordability play the biggest part in explaining this – many people with low incomes simply cannot afford to save at all, particularly when they are young and have dependent families (Kempson et al, 2000).

Several people did have savings accounts with a bank or building society, although these accounts were seldom in active use. In general, people believed that these accounts were only appropriate for saving relatively large amounts of money, rather than the couple of pounds a week that they could, at most, afford. Indeed, they said they would feel too embarrassed to go into a bank or building society to deposit such small amounts of cash. These concerns were almost certainly reinforced by the negative views that many people held about financial services providers in general.

In addition, savings accounts tended to be held with building societies rather than banks. As Barton Hill has no building society branches, it seems unlikely that residents would travel to the nearest branch to deposit a few pounds a week. In fact, it would almost cost that much to get there by public transport.

However, people did save in other ways. As we know, many people living on low incomes save informally (Kempson, 1998; Whyley et al, 2000), and several participants talked about saving money in jars, or giving money to a friend to keep for them.

As mentioned above, a number of participants were active credit union members. For these people, as in credit unions elsewhere, savings were most highly valued as a gateway to affordable loans. Little, if any, importance was attached to the dividends that their savings might yield (see Whyley et al, 2000). Finally, as described in the previous section, the Somali focus group participants all regularly saved at least £10 a week with a small community-based rotating savings and loans club.

Meeting the needs for savings and loans

Just as with personal banking services, there have been some innovative developments aimed at meeting the saving and borrowing needs of people living on low incomes. Most of these initiatives involve linking saving to loans – savings are used as collateral to keep the costs of the loans at a minimum. More recently, though, we have seen the development of new services offering access to low-cost loans that are not tied to savings.

Loan products

Given the problems of access outlined earlier, it seems likely that people living on low incomes will continue to be excluded from most sources of mainstream credit. In an effort to bridge the gap between mainstream credit and the high-cost alternative market, several community-based finance initiatives are being developed around the UK. Portsmouth Area Regeneration Trust (PART), launched in July 2000, is the first of these initiatives to become operational.

PART is a not-for-profit mutual organisation that has been designed to offer loans and other banking services to those excluded from mainstream financial institutions, and, in particular, to people living on low incomes. Loans are not, therefore, granted on the basis of a credit scoring system. Instead, applications are assessed according to the applicant's financial circumstances and ability to pay. As part of this, all applicants receive financial guidance and advice from PART staff.

PART plans to offer a variety of loans, covering a range of situations including:

- *Seedcorn loans*, to cover the cost of returning to work;
- *Consumption loans*, to cover the cost of essentials like children's clothing;
- *Fresh Start loans*, to refinance debt;
- *Micro-Enterprise loans*, for small businesses;
- *Energy loans*, to fund energy efficiency programmes for homeowners;
- *Home Improvement loans*, to enable elderly people to stay in their homes.

Loans are granted on a structure of planned repayment, with interest charged at a similar rate to that levied by the mainstream banks (around 15% for personal loans and 10% for home improvement loans). It does not, therefore, aim to offer cheap loans, but rather to provide access to loans at a reasonable rate. As previous research has indicated, people are prepared to meet the costs involved in delivering appropriate products, providing the charges are perceived to be reasonable (Kempson and Whyley, 1999). In the first four months of operation, PART has lent nearly £35,000 to 67 customers, giving an average loan size of about £500.

Breaking the link with moneylenders

Both local credit union members and community workers were interested in the role that organisations such as PART and credit unions could potentially play in providing cheaper alternatives to weekly-collected credit.

One way of achieving this is to set up a 'debt buy-out' facility. With the backing of some form of guarantee fund, the debt of the individual is 'bought out', transferring the money owed to PART or the credit union.

The conditions of credit union schemes usually require that, at the time of receiving a loan, the individual joins the credit union. The user then agrees to make a regular repayment which is split between an amount to be paid into credit union savings and an amount to repay the loan. The

Ely Debt Redemption Scheme (DRS)

Established with a grant of £3,000 from South Glamorgan County Council in 1993, the scheme offers immediate help to families facing imminent loss of a major social asset such as accommodation, gas, electricity or water, provided that help can be successfully delivered for a sum of £500 or less.

Individuals are referred to the scheme from the specialist money advice worker of the local Citizens Advice Bureau. In successful referrals, the individual's debt is 'bought out', leaving the money owed to the DRS itself. At the time of receiving a loan, the individual is also required to join the credit union. The amount repaid is divided between the loan repayment and savings. (From Drakeford and Sachdev, forthcoming.)

idea is that, once the credit union loan has been repaid, the user will hopefully have sufficient savings to borrow from the credit union rather than from more expensive sources. A scheme of this type was set up by Ely credit union to help families facing imminent loss of an essential service, such as accommodation, gas or electricity.

Given the prevalence of licensed and unlicensed moneylenders operating in Barton Hill, it is not surprising that local workers at the select committee were keen to develop this type of scheme. In order to achieve this, though, the credit union would first have to secure adequate finance.

Savings and loans schemes

When asked to describe how they would ideally like to save, focus group participants identified the following key features:

* a secure means of saving small amounts, possibly depositing loose change;
* a routine to their saving – this might involve sorting out all their 20 pence pieces at the end of the day, or going to a credit union or other savings institution on a set day;
* they did not want to be able to dip into their savings for small amounts whenever they ran short of cash, so access to savings needed to be fairly limited;
* they wanted to be able to save locally;
* they liked the idea of saving to gain access to low-cost loans.

There are a growing number of savings and loans schemes that appear to meet these requirements.

Credit unions are probably the best-known providers of savings and loans schemes in the UK. While keen to move away from the image of the 'poor person's bank', credit unions nonetheless have the potential to meet many of the saving and borrowing needs of low-income households. This is equally true of more recent entrants to this market, such as the *New Horizons* scheme, which was established in 1997 by Cambridge Housing Society, in partnership with Cambridge Building Society.

Although different in structure and operation, credit unions and the *New Horizons* scheme both serve a dual purpose – to encourage regular

New Horizons savings and loans scheme

New Horizons was developed by Cambridge Housing Society (CHS) in partnership with Cambridge Building Society (CBS). Launched in 1997, the scheme is open to CHS tenants, their resident partners and children.

Underpinning the scheme is a Guarantee Fund of £25,000, deposited by CHS with the CBS. This enables CHS tenants to borrow from teh CBS without credit scoring, as well as receiving an enhanced rate of interest on their savings.

The scheme offers three main products:

* *Savings* account;
* *Main Loan* account, which allows savers to borrow up to four times the amount they have in savings, at an interest rate of 0.95% above base rate (currently 6.95%). The maximum amount for a first loan is £1,000, rising to £2,000 for second and subsequent loans. Loans are repaid over 24 to 36 months;
* *Handy Loan* account, which allows savings account holders to borrow up to £150 without actually having to save beforehand. Loans are repaid over 12 months at the same rate of interest as the main loan account.

saving against which members can borrow at a reasonable rate of interest.

Community credit unions appear to have two distinct advantages over mainstream financial providers in terms of meeting the savings needs of people in Barton Hill. First, they have a local presence: they are run by, and for, the community. Second, they *encourage* small-scale savings – recent research found that the majority of credit union members living on low incomes saved between £1 and £5 a week (Whyley et al, 2000).

As with credit union accounts, the *New Horizons* savings account can be opened with an initial deposit of £1. Members can pay in or withdraw money using a passbook from any of the 21 branches of Cambridge Building Society in and around Cambridge. The account currently offers savers a fairly competitive gross interest rate of just over 4%. But for many members of schemes such as these, saving is not an end in itself. Rather, it is the route to accessible, affordable and appropriate loans.

Unlike mainstream lenders, applications for loans are not credit scored (Cambridge Building Society does, however, check for current bankruptcy with a credit reference agency). Instead, applications are usually assessed on people's financial circumstances and their ability to make repayments. The 'credit facility' open to members depends on the level of their savings. Credit union members can typically borrow two or three times the amount they have saved; members of the *New Horizons* scheme can borrow up to four times their savings.

The loans offered by these schemes are also cheaper than the other sources of credit typically available to people on low incomes. The annual interest rate for credit unions is fixed at 12.68%, while the *New Horizons* scheme aims to charge 0.95% above base rate, which currently equates to 6.95% APR.

For many people, however, the drawback of these schemes is the pre-saving requirement. Quite simply, they may be unable to save on a regular basis, or they may need money straightaway. Having identified these problems among their tenants, the *New Horizons* scheme developed an 'instant access' loan (called the 'Handy Loan') which is currently being piloted.

Applicants can apply for a loan of up to £150 without having to save beforehand, although they do have to open a *New Horizons* savings account. There have been similar developments among credit unions.

When discussed at the select committee, the idea of 'instant access' loans was fairly popular among local residents. Several credit union members, however, felt that the link between saving and borrowing was vital to encourage people to repay their loans:

> "… you don't know everybody in Barton Hill, and you don't know whether they'll actually pay that loan back. Whereas if they've got savings, it encourages you to save and to pay it back."

On balance, *New Horizons* and credit unions appear to come close to meeting the needs identified by the focus group participants. Making them readily available to the people of Barton Hill may prove more challenging.

Initiatives such as the *New Horizons* saving and loan scheme have a great deal to commend them. Although Barton Hill has very few housing association tenants, the role of Cambridge Housing Society could be played by an organisation such as the local authority or city council. A greater problem may be the lack of a local building society to enter into such a partnership. Of course, a bank could fulfil this role just as well, but, as yet, none of the main high street banks has expressed an interest in doing so.

With regard to community credit unions, Barton Hill is within the common bond area of the Money-go-Round credit union, which was registered with the Registrar of Friendly Societies in July 1999, and covers the whole of inner-city Bristol. At the end of June 2000, Money-go-Round had 186 adult and 50 junior members. It has six collection points, including a weekly one in Barton Hill.

At present, though, only a very small proportion of Barton Hill residents are members of Money-go-Round. Therefore, in order for the credit union to meet the saving and borrowing needs of the wider community, it needs to undergo considerable expansion. The problems it faces in doing so are common to most community credit unions in the UK. Put simply, credit unions need to move towards a 'virtuous circle' of development – they have to attract more savings, which will lead to bigger loans, which will lead to higher income, bigger reserves, more members, more savings, and so on (Jones, 1998).

In order to achieve this 'virtuous circle', a number of conditions have to exist, or be fostered, within credit unions. In particular, they need strong leadership and professional management; a core group of active volunteers; effective organisation and promotional work; appropriate operational resources; IT infrastructure and appropriate IT skills among workers; the capacity to offer a range of high quality services; and good business sense and planning skills (Conaty and Mayo, undated; Feloy and Payne, 1999; HM Treasury, 1999c).

The establishment of a Credit Union Central Services Organisation (as recommended by the Treasury-led Credit Union Taskforce; HM Treasury, 1999c) could help credit unions achieve some or all of these conditions. A draft Business Plan for the Central Services Organisation is currently under consideration. Even if this is agreed, it could be some time before the benefits are felt by Money-go-Round and the people of Barton Hill.

There was, however, a notable lack of enthusiasm for the development of the local credit union among members who attended the select committee. Extended opening hours and access to savings through cash machines held no great appeal for them. They liked the fact that they could only withdraw their savings once a week when the collection point was open, as this effectively restricted their access and made it more difficult to withdraw the savings on impulse. Nor were they interested in the expansion of products and services: they preferred the credit union simply to offer savings and loans.

As with banking services, what people appeared to want was something local and something simple. If it is the preferred provider, the challenge for the local credit union will be to achieve its own 'virtuous circle' of development while retaining the aspects of the current service that people living on low incomes most value. Ideally, local residents should have the choice between a credit union and some other form of savings and loans scheme, as some people simply do not want to become members of a credit union (Whyley et al, 2000).

Islam-compliant savings and loans products

At present, there are no Islamic banks authorised in the UK, nor are there any commercial or community-based organisations that offer financial services appropriate to the needs of Muslim people living on low incomes.

There are, however, a number of possibilities for providing products suitable for Muslim consumers in the future. The ABCUL is currently exploring the feasibility of developing Islamic credit unions in the UK, as recommended by PAT 14 (HM Treasury, 1999a).

The Swedish JAK Bank also offers an interesting model for providing interest-free savings and loans. Local Muslim residents in Barton Hill confirmed that these types of products would comply with Islamic teaching and, perhaps more importantly, that they would be prepared to use them.

JAK Bank, Sweden

Established in Sweden as a cooperative savings and loans association in 1965, the JAK Bank was granted official bank status by the Swedish government in December 1997. The main function of the bank is to provide members with interest-free savings loans. To this end, no interest is paid on savings, and only an administration fee is taken for loans. It also has plans to introduce an interest-free profit/loss-sharing loan instrument used widely in Muslim countries which is specifically geared towards financing businesses. (From http://www.jak.se/)

5

Financial education and information

Previous chapters of this report have focused on needs for particular financial products and services in Barton Hill, and identified the most appropriate options for meeting them. Ensuring that these products are available to people living in Barton Hill will, undoubtedly, improve their access to financial services. Yet simply making them available will not overcome the problem of financial exclusion. It is also necessary to ensure that people feel confident in their ability to make decisions about financial services and to use them effectively. More importantly, there is a need to overcome the widespread mistrust of, and antipathy towards, financial institutions among people in Barton Hill. Without this, it is extremely unlikely that people will take out financial products, however appropriate or accessible they are. Consequently, exploring ways of improving levels of financial literacy is a key factor in addressing financial exclusion in areas such as Barton Hill. In many respects, it is also the biggest challenge.

Needs for financial education and information in Barton Hill

Focus groups with local people highlighted a number of issues relating to financial literacy:

- a widespread lack of knowledge about financial products and services;
- a lack of basic money management skills, among young people and those who were setting up home for the first time;
- a strong and widespread antipathy towards the financial services industry, which was a key barrier to their use of financial products.

Lack of knowledge

A lack of knowledge of financial products and services was an issue for everyone who took part in the focus groups. However, it was most noticeable among young people who had just left school – largely because of their limited experience of using financial products – and among the Somali women, due to the additional language and cultural barriers they faced in engaging with the financial services industry. However, even people who were making some use of financial products demonstrated only a limited understanding of them.

A number of gaps in people's knowledge and understanding impeded their use of financial products and undermined their confidence in engaging with the financial services industry. In particular, people lacked a detailed understanding of:

- everyday financial products;
- the factors that determine access to financial products;
- financial services institutions;
- where to turn for information or advice on financial services.

Financial products

Lack of knowledge about financial products was widespread and applied, to a varying degree, to all financial products and services. People's knowledge was very much limited to their personal experience. Nobody who took part in the focus groups had a clear knowledge map of financial services provision that they could draw on.

Current accounts were the most commonly used financial product among focus group participants. Even so, they tended to be utilised only at a very basic level and, consequently, were still surrounded by misconceptions. For example, many people confused current accounts and savings accounts, and some felt that a current account was only of value if you had money to save. Few people were aware of the different types of current account that are available. Many were also unaware of the range of facilities attached to current accounts, and of how to gain access to them.

In addition, there was a great deal of uncertainty about the extent and nature of charges that could be imposed on people using a current account. Few people knew the exact circumstances in which charges were levied; those who did had found out through bitter experience. As a result, several misconceptions had developed and become received wisdom. One person, for example, thought they would be charged simply for keeping money in an account. Others thought that all bank customers were charged if their account balance fell below a specified level. Another believed that banks charged customers for using facilities such as direct debits and standing orders. It was also not uncommon for people to think that they would be charged if they wanted to close an account, particularly if they were planning to open one with another bank. In fact, few people knew how to go about closing an account and often simply changed banks without closing their original accounts.

Most people were more knowledgeable about sources of credit, largely because the need to borrow money was fairly widespread among the focus group participants. However, although most people had a fairly good idea of the range of credit products available, they were much less knowledgeable about the interest rates charged on different types of credit and by different providers. Many, particularly the young people, were also unaware of the conditions attached to different types of loans and the consequences of non-payment.

There was a particular lack of knowledge in relation to savings and pensions.

Most people's awareness of the range of savings products was fairly limited, again especially among young people. Apart from bank or building society savings accounts, only Post Office

accounts and National Savings were mentioned. Very few people knew about Individual Savings Accounts (ISAs) and understanding of them was poor. Although some people said that interest rates were important to them in choosing a savings account, few knew what rates of interest were available with different types of savings product. There was also confusion about the terms and conditions attached to different accounts and facilities.

Focus group participants were, however, least knowledgeable about pensions. In general, they did not fully understand the consequences of not having a private pension. Very few knew how to go about taking out a private pension and Stakeholder Pensions had made little impact. The small number who had occupational pensions did not always understand how to transfer them if they changed jobs. Similarly, others who had paid into employment-based pension schemes that had been frozen when they left their job did not know how to go about accessing the money held in them.

Gaining access to financial products

Another area of confusion related to the factors that determine access to financial products and, again, misconceptions were common. Very few people had a clear understanding of the processes involved in credit scoring or risk assessment, or the reason why banks require particular forms of identification before they can open a current account for a new customer. As a result, people tended to believe that they lived in an area that was redlined or that their address had been blacklisted due to the outstanding debts of a previous occupant. This is, in fact, very unlikely (see Chapters 3 and 4). In addition, very few of the people who thought they were blacklisted knew how to go about clearing their name.

Providers of financial products

Many of the focus group participants lacked awareness of the organisations that provide financial products and services and, in particular, how to go about choosing between them.

Most people's awareness of financial services providers was limited to banks and credit companies. Providers of insurance, savings or pension products were much less widely known. This was particularly the case among young people. One young man said that if he was trying to get insurance he would simply look for the biggest advert in the Yellow Pages, on the grounds that only successful companies could afford to place prominent adverts.

Knowledge of non-commercial provision was also very limited. A high proportion of people did not know that there was a credit union operating in the area. Similarly, many people who rented their homes from the local authority were unaware that the council offered home contents insurance through an 'insure-with-rent' scheme.

Sources of information and advice

Finally, despite the fact that many people were confused about financial products they had little idea of where they could seek advice.

Most people thought that the only place they could get information about products was from providers themselves, particularly from bank managers. For advice, people generally agreed that they would turn to family members or friends.

Equally, they had little idea of how to find out about their rights as consumers of financial products and, in particular, where and how they could complain about the services they were using.

Money management skills

Focus group participants also identified a need for training in the basic money management skills required to effectively manage a household budget:

> "You've only got to look 'round, there's a lot of illiterate people 'round. They're not illiterate as people but illiterate financially. They don't even know how to take care of their money. They need people to come down here and educate people like this."

This was identified as a particular need for people who were setting up home for the first time – particularly young, lone parents. Many adults felt that they had been unprepared for financial independence when they first set up home:

> "I think you learn a lot more when you leave school, money management wise, than when you're at school. Because all

this maths ... percentages and algebra and that lot, what's that got to do with paying your bank? ... I don't think that's got anything to do with actual, you know, money management or anything."

> "I didn't have a clue about money or anything when I was at school because there wasn't anything around [to teach me]. And then when I actually moved out there were all these bills coming in and I was like, 'I'm not going to be able to get the money to pay them'."

Consequently, they were forced to learn by trial and error:

> "You end up getting yourself into debt don't you? Then you realise you've done it, you should have done it right from the beginning really."

This feeling was echoed by the young people who took part in the research, who were not confident in their ability to manage household finances:

> "I couldn't handle it. Because my money just comes and I blow it on things."

They felt their schooling should have better prepared them for the difficulties of financial independence:

> "They don't tell you actually how scary it's going to be, I don't think. Because when I left school I thought it was just going to be easy ... but it's not at all, it's definitely not easy.... It just gets on top of you and they don't teach you that in school, so you have to deal with it."

Consequently, the young people who took part in the focus groups were expecting to have to develop money management skills by learning from their mistakes.

Financial antipathy

Underpinning the more specific concerns outlined above was a deep and widespread antipathy towards financial institutions. The main focus of this was the mistrust of banks outlined in Chapter 3. However, this antipathy applied to some degree to all financial institutions.

Many focus group participants felt that financial institutions did not understand, and were not interested in meeting, the needs of 'ordinary people'. This is illustrated by the following exchange between three women in one of the groups:

> "They'll cater for people who've got their own properties, they'll do all they can for them. But not for the likes of us."

> "Not for the likes of us."

> "Because as soon as you say you're a council tenant and you come from Barton Hill it's, 'Sorry'."

Consequently, they had developed a strong suspicion of them, assuming that financial institutions were interested only in making money out of them by 'ripping them off'. Their lack of knowledge of financial products and limited experience in dealing with providers made people feel particularly vulnerable to misinformation and exploitation.

As a result, many were wary of becoming involved with financial institutions and found it difficult to perceive them as trustworthy. This made them sceptical about whether they would actually want to deal with financial institutions, even if they were offering appropriate and accessible products. It is this mistrust of financial services providers that is likely to present the biggest obstacle to promoting financial inclusion.

There was some evidence (particularly from the select committee) that this antipathy was even greater for men than it was for women. This would certainly be consistent with the considerable body of research evidence that points to women having the most responsibility for managing the household finances in low-income households. This study did not, however, set out to explore this particular aspect of financial exclusion, but it would clearly merit further investigation.

Meeting the needs for financial education and information

Focus group participants felt that the need for financial education and information in Barton Hill could be met in two main ways. First, by providing basic training in money management skills; second, through the provision of a source of independent advice and explanation on financial products and services.

Training in money management skills

Most of the adults who took part in the focus groups believed that there was a need for money management skills to be taught at school, preferably from a young age:

> "I think if you try and start when they're 14 or 15, if they want to learn they learn, if they don't they don't. But if you teach them when they're younger, and they're sort of 5, 6, 7, that sort of age group, I reckon then they've got it sort of brainwashed and they'll learn."

By teaching children how to manage their money from an early age, the adult focus group participants felt that they would leave school with an ability to cope with a household budget.

However, evidence indicates that teaching money management skills at school is not, by itself, sufficient. The young people who took part in the research believed strongly that, to be successful, this teaching must be relevant to people's needs and circumstances. They felt that schools should teach children about saving and budgeting, and how to prepare for working life. Other aspects of money management, such as borrowing and insurance, do not become relevant until after people have left school and, consequently, need to be taught later on in life.

In addition, it was clear from the focus group with young people that, despite being provided with some personal finance education at school, many 'fall through the net' and leave school without having acquired these skills. Several of the young focus group participants admitted that they had not paid attention to personal finance education at school. They felt that it was not taught in an interesting way and that teachers were not always well-equipped to provide this type of education. Furthermore, many had not realised the importance of developing money management skills until after they had left school.

Finally, it is also important to recognise that young people who are excluded from school or who play truant from lessons will also miss out on the opportunity to learn about money management.

Independent advice and explanation

Focus group participants expressed a need for an independent source of advice and explanation. A service such as this could provide them with genuinely impartial information about financial products and services:

> "Someone who will understand and give them all the information they need because ... they never – even banks – they don't give you the information that you actually need. They only give you the information that you want to hear, so it would be nice if someone told you what you're getting yourself into before you do."

However, it would not simply provide them with information, but also help them to understand and assess the implications of the information they received. This would help them to make more effective decisions and ensure that they were aware of all the relevant facts before they made any decisions.

An organisation offering this type of advice would have to understand the needs and circumstances of the people they were dealing with:

> "Somebody that, you know, that's been there, done that. That understands where you're coming from, that will tell you maybe that this is not an option that you want to choose."

Such an organisation would also have to be trustworthy, so that people could be confident about the advice they received. One of the Somali women described it as, "on your side, rather than just making money for themselves".

Given these requirements, people did not believe that this advice service could be offered by the financial services industry, because it was only motivated by self-interest and profit. Equally, they felt that neither central nor local government could be trusted to provide such a service, as "the left hand often does not know what the right hand is doing". They were also sceptical about whether they could rely on the FSA's comparative information, as they believed that this information

would have to be gathered from financial service providers who might not give honest information to the FSA. In reality this is a problem that can be overcome, although it is significant that people on the margins of financial services did not believe that it could be.

The general consensus was that this type of independent advice service could only be offered by a non-commercial organisation, such as a Citizens Advice Bureau. There are, however, potential problems.

Unless such a service restricted itself to giving generic advice it would need to meet all the regulatory requirements on financial services advice-giving, just like other independent financial advisers. Yet all the evidence is that people wanted fairly specific advice about which product would be most appropriate for their particular circumstances, rather than generic advice about a range of possibilities.

Options for meeting the needs for financial education and information

The needs for training in money management skills that were expressed by people in Barton Hill could, potentially, be met in a variety of ways. It was more difficult, however, to identify any existing options for providing the type of independent advice and explanation service that focus group participants needed. The solutions that were identified are outlined briefly below.

Training in money management skills

Recent interest in the issue of personal finance education has stimulated the development of a range of projects, courses and initiatives aimed at promoting financial literacy among particular groups of people. Most of this activity, however, has been aimed at school children and young people.

School-based schemes

The provision of money management training in schools has been improving. From September 2000, personal finance education in England has been enshrined in the National Curriculum at all four Key Stages as part of Personal, Social and Health Education (PSHE) and Citizenship (the situation is different in Scotland, Wales and Northern Ireland). This aims to promote 'financial capability' in all school children to "enable children to make informed judgements and to take effective decisions regarding the use and management of money in their present and adult lives" (DfEE, 2000b). Financial capability in schools has three core elements:

- financial knowledge and understanding;
- financial skills and competence;
- financial responsibility.

The Department for Education and Employment (DfEE) has published detailed guidance for teachers, including how and where financial capability fits in with PSHE and Citizenship teaching, the best methods of teaching financial capability, and the level of financial capability that children should develop at each Key Stage (DfEE, 2000b, 2000c).

In addition, the National Curriculum is supported by a wide range of initiatives and resources, provided by financial institutions, credit unions, charities and consumer and regulatory bodies. These include websites and education packs featuring information, worksheets, quizzes, 'real life' activities and notes for teachers, as well as printed information and more practical initiatives such as school-based banks and savings schemes.

Although undoubtedly important, money management training in schools was not central to this research, which has focused on ways of meeting the needs of adults and those who fall through the educational net.

Schemes for adults

Although there are a number of options for teaching money management skills to adults, this level of provision is less organised, more localised, and tends to be targeted at specific client groups (see DfEE, 2000a). An assessment of the various options available suggests that needs for training in money management skills among adults in Barton Hill could be met in two principal ways. First, existing school-based educational programmes and initiatives could be adapted for use with adults. Second, a range of taught courses, aimed specifically at adults, has been developed by voluntary and community groups, credit unions, charities and advice

Face-to-Face with Finance

The *Face-to-Face* programme consists of a series of 10 modules which can stand alone or be used together.

- basic banking
- cards and card services
- enterprise
- tender
- credit worthy?
- it's your life
- EMU
- fresher finance
- work experience
- teacher placement

Each module is made up of a number of individual activities and is supported by high quality support materials and software, and a handbook containing all the information necessary to deliver the programme. Most of the information and activities contained in the modules are not age-related and the materials could be made available to adults.

agencies. A similar course could be developed in Barton Hill.

One of the most comprehensive school-based personal finance education programmes is *Face-to-Face with Finance*, run by NatWest Bank. *Face-to-Face* is an internet-based resource that enables teachers to download teaching materials for use with 11- to 19-year-olds free of charge. The materials involve practical and active learning experiences, and the programme is supported by a curriculum guide to show teachers how the materials link to other subject areas, as well as case studies of how the materials have been utilised in other schools. In addition, NatWest Bank provides a trained member of staff to work with teachers and provide back up information and support. Since its introduction in 1994, more than 2,000 schools have registered to use the scheme and it has won several awards.

Residents were initially sceptical about the *Face-to-Face* programme and this is likely to be a result of their antipathy towards all financial institutions, and banks in particular. A few local residents expressed concern that the scheme would encourage people to use financial products, particularly credit facilities, that were not in their best interests. They did eventually accept that the programme was intended to be an awareness-raising, rather than a marketing, exercise. It is likely, however, that financial antipathy might put people off using a training programme that they associate with a bank or other institution.

The fact that *Face-to-Face* is a computer-based programme was also considered to be potentially problematic by residents. This made it inaccessible for people without access to a computer. In addition, many of the local residents were unable to use computers, and so would need help to use the programme. Consequently, they were unsure whether it could, in practice, be made available to people in Barton Hill, as it would mean providing access to both computers and computing support. At present, Barton Hill Settlement is the only potential provider of these facilities, as the area does not even have a library through which they could be made available.

Some workers, on the other hand, felt that *Face-to-Face* might be too 'institutionally driven' to meet the financial literacy needs of everyone in Barton Hill. Although they thought it could be useful for people who already had some financial knowledge to find out more about the financial services industry, some felt that the course might not be practical enough to meet the needs of those who were more disengaged. Finally, one resident, who was both visually and hearing impaired, was concerned that the materials may not be adapted for people with these sorts of disabilities. In fact, the *Face-to-Face* student materials are available in both large print and Braille, although the teaching materials are not.

Despite these concerns, most select committee members thought that adapting the *Face-toFace* programme for adults was a good idea. Both residents and workers felt that it was useful for parents to be aware of what their children were learning about financial services. In addition, people thought that *Face-to-Face* could be used for parents and children to learn together. Indeed, several of the residents wanted to use something like *Face-to-Face* to teach their children about finances.

The main benefit of *Face-to-Face* was that people could work through it fairly independently and without needing to sign up for a formal course. One resident, in recognition of the increasing range of financial products that are delivered via the internet, felt that computers were the most appropriate medium for learning about them:

"The computer programme [is good] because at the end of the day, the computer is linked to getting financial services ... it's all technology these days."

Nearly all local residents who took part in the select committee thought that they would sign up for this programme if it was available to them.

One of the most innovative taught courses in money management skills for adults has been developed in Coventry by Willenhall Community Education Department, alongside Willenhall Community Money Advice Centre.

A key element of this course is the link between basic skills and financial education. One of the people involved in developing the course explained that, without this link, many people are unable to apply the skills they learn. Consequently, a course was developed incorporating basic literacy and numeracy as well as money management.

A crucial factor in the success of the course is that it is delivered jointly by a basic skills worker and an advice worker. This ensures that courses are taught at the most appropriate level, as well as covering the key elements of money management on which information and advice is most often required. This link between financial education

Willenhall Community Money Advice Centre

The advice centre set up a money management training course because they found that many of the people in debt that they were helping, returned a few months later with the same problems. The course is taught in 10 two-hour weekly sessions:

- The causes of debt
- Where does your money go?
- What do we need to spend money on?
- Benefit entitlements and how to claim
- The cost of credit
- Cheaper ways of borrowing money
- Consumer rights
- Complaining by letter
- Negotiating by telephone
- Feedback

It has been delivered in a variety of contexts, including in hostels for the homeless and through a mental health charity.

and basic skills teaching is endorsed by the Basic Skills Agency.

Local residents and workers were very interested in the type of taught course run by Willenhall Community Money Advice Centre. Residents liked the idea of face-to-face teaching and being able to ask questions, and felt that the topics covered were both useful and relevant. In addition, because the course had been designed in response to local needs, workers felt that the content was "underpinned by the demands of practical life in the community".

The main concern they expressed related to the difficulties they could foresee in setting up the course amidst "all the lack of interest and apathy here". Several residents felt that a 10-week course was too long and that there would be a high drop out rate. They thought six weeks was the maximum period that people could realistically be expected to attend. A few also thought that it might be more appropriate to run each module independently, so people could attend only the sessions that were relevant to them. Local workers believed that once people had been "hooked into training" by a short course or seminar it would be easier to find out what topics were most relevant to them, and so encourage them to attend further courses.

In general, local residents did not feel that there would be a stigma attached to attending a money management course delivered through a debt counselling service. This was largely because they felt that debt was such a common problem there was no need to feel embarrassed or ashamed about it. In addition, people saw going to a debt counselling service for training in money management skills as taking a positive step to help themselves. Most of the women did not think that they would feel differently about signing up for training at a debt counselling service if they were not in debt:

> "I don't think I would, because you're there to learn about it, to save yourself getting into debt."

It was not clear whether the men would be equally comfortable about attending a training course at a debt counselling centre if they were not in debt. All the select committee participants said they would sign up for this kind of course if it was available in Barton Hill.

Independent source of advice and explanation

A number organisations, such as the FSA, the National Association of Citizen's Advice Bureaux (NACAB) and the Office of Fair Trading (OFT), have websites that provide independent information on financial products and services for customers. However, focus group participants made it clear that information alone is not sufficient to ensure effective decision making. Consequently, ways of fulfilling this need remain something of a grey area.

We were, however, unable to identify any examples of projects or initiatives that offer independent advice and explanation on financial products and services, although one was in the process of being set up by Birmingham Settlement. They have recognised that this new service is quite distinct from the money advice and debt counselling service pioneered by the Settlement. They plan, therefore, to work closely with local independent financial advisers from the commercial sector – on much the same basis as advice agencies have worked with lawyers who are prepared to do *pro bono* work. In this way, they can bring in new expertise and also comply with regulatory requirements. They have also recognised that they cannot offer a new service from their existing resources. Both these points are important. It is unrealistic to expect existing advice agencies to develop a new service, requiring additional expertise, without extra funding.

Priorities for the future

All local residents and workers thought that it was important that some form of training in money management skills be made available to adults in Barton Hill. There was a strong view that it was important to enable adults – particularly parents – to develop these skills so that they could reinforce the personal finance education that their children received at school:

> "It's very important to educate children, but isn't it equally important to educate adults?"

> "It's just that if you train the adults then the children are going to learn from the parents. Rather than training the children to train the parents."

Residents were fairly evenly divided, over whether they thought the *Face-to-Face with Finance* programme or the taught course was the best option. In fact, both residents and workers thought that each would be insufficient on its own and that the best option would be to make both available, to provide a multifaceted approach to training in financial literacy. In this context, *Face-to-Face* would teach people the basics they needed to use financial products and services, while a taught course would focus on more practical topics such as running a household budget and priorities for bill payment. There was also a view, however, that any sort of training would be better than none. As one person commented, "With knowledge you can only go higher".

Local workers thought that training in financial literacy should be provided through partnerships between organisations that already exist in Barton Hill, such as the credit union or the Post Office. In fact, credit unions already have a responsibility to provide training and information for their members. In addition, the not-for-profit money advice centre that covers Barton Hill is "committed to exploring the possibility of preventative work, rather than sticking plasters on".

Despite the fact that local residents thought training in money management skills would help to overcome financial exclusion in Barton Hill, they still perceived a need for the independent advice and explanation service discussed in the focus groups. While training might provide them with a better understanding of financial matters, they felt strongly that they would still need help with decision making.

However, all the residents agreed, albeit reluctantly, that if they were forced to choose between training in money management skills and an advice and explanation service they would choose the training. This would at least equip them with sufficient knowledge to ask the correct questions when they were considering taking out financial products or services.

6

The needs of micro-businesses

People who have had an insecure work history often see self-employment as a route into work or into more secure employment. But the types of micro-businesses that are set up by people in deprived communities often face problems of access to financial services that are every bit as great as those faced by individuals. As a consequence, there has been a strong policy focus on improving access to financial services by micro-businesses (usually defined as those with between one and five employees and a modest turnover). Both the Treasury and the Bank of England are taking an active interest in this area (HM Treasury, 1999b; Bank of England, 2000).

One of the focus groups was specifically recruited to explore the unmet needs for financial services among self-employed people. These were typically people who had been trading in the informal economy before 'going legitimate'. This meant either working as self-employed while claiming benefit and not declaring their earnings, or being self-employed but not registering for either income tax or national insurance. They were what the banks would call 'lifestyle businesses'; that is, they aimed to make a living by being self-employed in the service sector but had no plans for long-term expansion. They had been drawn to self-employment as an alternative to insecure work for someone else. The term 'lifestyle business' implies something rather more glamorous than the types of service businesses they ran (window-cleaning, painting/decorating) or their motivations for doing so.

In addition, some of the Somali women were attracted to the idea of self-employment. For them, starting a small business was both an alternative to claiming Income Support and a way of making financial provision for the future that was in keeping with the teaching of Islam. Their

aspirations were also modest – setting up a photography business or possibly opening a small shop.

Banking

The self-employed people all had bank accounts, although they tended to use one bank account for both their business and their personal finances. One man not only mixed personal and business finances, but also had a joint account with his wife who was self-employed as well. Other studies have shown that this pattern of mixing business and personal finances is common among micro-businesses (Whyley, 1998; Kempson and Jones, 2000). It can, however, have serious consequences should the business begin to fail.

In most cases, no consideration had been given to opening a separate bank account. Although one man, who did not trade under his own name, had been told by his bank that he would have to open a business account to receive cheques made out to his trading name:

> "... it wasn't a problem paying them into the bank [at first], and then they changed their policy, and they simply told me that they would not pay [business] cheques any more unless I set up a business account – and then they would charge me for every cheque I paid into the bank ... so I deal as much in cash as I can. The tax man tells me it would be a lot easier if I dealt completely with cheques and didn't work for cash, but that would increase my costs astronomically."

Like this man, self-employed people often avoided business accounts if they could, because of the charges that are normally associated with them. But they were also critical of the charges that they incurred using a personal account. These included charges for inadvertently overdrawing and bounced cheques, which were all too common with accounts that were used for combined business and personal purposes.

Charges for the use of cash machines were a particular bugbear – especially for self-employed people whose work meant that they were peripatetic:

> "I am with [name of bank] and they have two cash machines; one in Clifton and one in [the city centre], and if I am in Fishponds what the hell do I do for money? I am forced into the situation of having to use something else and having to pay for it, so they are bringing in disloyalty charges. Then make sure there are [more cash machines] available, and I won't be disloyal."

This problem was highlighted in an earlier study of small business banking (Kempson and Jones, 2000).

There was a general feeling that greater centralisation and automation of banking had led to a less personal service and greater problems for people struggling to make a go of being self-employed:

> "My father was a builder ... and sometimes, during the winter, there was no work and the bank saw them through ... it was there to help and when times were plentiful it took it back ... it's not like that any more."

> "... with all this centralisation, there is nobody at the bank to say, 'Hold it, a cheque is coming in ... it's due in tomorrow, let's give him a temporary overdraft'. That's not happening."

When asked if they had thought about changing banks, the general view seemed to be that, as all banks are developing in the same way, there would be little point. In any case, some people did not think it would be easy to transfer, based on their earlier experiences of having applications for current accounts turned down.

Access to credit

On the whole, there had been little need for start-up capital among those who were already self-employed – mainly because most of them had started trading in the informal economy and had gradually built up their businesses to the point where they could 'go legitimate'. This had included doing self-employed work while claiming benefit and/or not declaring an income for tax purposes:

> "Basically I had everything already, because what I was actually doing was legalising what I was already doing, so I didn't need start-up money."

Difficulties arose, however, with getting small amounts of working capital once the business had 'gone legitimate'. This would undoubtedly have been compounded by their lack of business banking relationships – as noted above, most kept little or no separation between their personal and business finances.

One man had, in the past, succeeded in getting a loan for business equipment by taking out a personal loan, which had been arranged through his bank manager with whom he had a very good relationship:

> "We told the bank manager that basically we wanted to buy some new equipment, but we'd say it was for a car and for a new kitchen back door. And by doing that, he knew what it was for, but by telling lies on the form we had no trouble at all."

Since then things have changed, even for those with a good relationship with their bank manager:

> "We are on first name terms, but it is not down to the bank manager any more. His input mattered a lot when we got the first loan, and policies change. You can't ring the local bank now, you have got to ring the call centre, if they deem it worthy, they might put you through to the bank."

In fact, there was, again, a general feeling that centralisation of banking had made things more difficult for the self-employed. This applies particularly to those who use only personal banking but also, to an increasing extent, to business customers too (Kempson and Whyley, 1998a):

> "When I needed some money a few years back, the bank very happily gave me a loan and that was no problem. And they wrote to me 18 months later saying I could have another loan, better interest rates ... to pay off this existing loan ... so I went down and chatted to the bank manager, he thought it was a brilliant idea. Head office turned it down, they said I couldn't have a loan."

A freelance disk jockey had his van broken into and all his equipment stolen. He asked the bank for a £2,000 loan to replace it, but was turned down. He struggled to keep his business going using a domestic CD player until he got together enough money to buy replacements. Another man had applied for a loan to attend a training course. He, too, was turned down, and so had been unable to get the training he felt he needed.

Experiences such as these led self-employed people to feel that it was pointless even applying for a bank loan:

> "Basically, I am not classed as credit worthy, so I don't go to my bank for anything. There is no point, being as when I have asked for anything it has always been turned down."

There was, therefore, a generally held belief that banks are just not interested in having some types of small businesses as customers:

> "What I have generally found is that banks are really not interested in lending you money unless you have got money."

> "But is part of it also because it's small, because it is a small business, are they interested? I mean my business, if I turn over £20,000 a year I'd be delighted, absolutely delighted, so why should they be that interested in me?"

The Somali women who were interested in the possibility of setting up a small business were also doubtful that any bank would be prepared to lend them money. In their case, however, the greater problem was the lack of Islam-compliant loans.

Because most people in Barton Hill rent their homes, this too was felt to be a barrier to getting a business bank loan as they would have nothing to offer as security. Also, the most mobile of the local authority tenants would find it very difficult indeed to pass the credit screening of banks. A further hurdle was the lack of certified accounts, especially where people worked for cash-in-hand. Consequently, there was a pervasive feeling that the odds were stacked against micro-businesses in areas such as Barton Hill:

> "I think the objective of ... being self-employed ... is to be able to put myself in a position where ... I am able to get a credit rating. So it is like you have all these hurdles in the way, and they are not even consciously putting them there, they are just there. So there is no way through, really."

When asked specifically what questions they would want to put to banks, two key issues emerged. First, improved access to modest amounts of finance:

> "Well basically what can they do for somebody like me? All the money I earn is probably going to be a lot less than somebody doing a normal job. Is there anything they can actually offer me? Because I don't want to borrow vast sums of money off them, I would like a £500 overdraft, or something like that, and that is all I want from them."

Second, a more personal service through bank branches:

> "I would like to see less centralisation ... so whilst you see and know the people in the local branch, they have no responsibility, the bank manager hasn't. He might have the title of bank manager, but he's just chief clerk now ... it's not for the customer's benefit, it's for the bank's benefit. Instead of making £19 million, they want to make £25 million a year."

Given the pressures on banks from their shareholders, neither aspiration is likely to be realisable. It is this gap that the not-for-profit micro-lenders have sought to fill. These are described in more detail below.

Other financial services

Compared with banking and access to business finance, the self-employed people were much less concerned about access to other financial services. Access to insurance – both liability and creditor – was not a particular problem. Following criticism of insurance companies, self-employed people no longer face the difficulties getting creditor insurance that was previously the case (Ford and Kempson, 1997; Kempson et al, 1999).

Other research has shown that retailers in high-crime neighbourhoods such as Barton Hill face difficulty in obtaining insurance to cover burglary or vandalism (Kempson and Whyley, 1998a). Although no retailers took part in the focus group, the manager of Bristol Enterprise Development Fund (BEDF) told us that such problems do exist.

The low level of pension holding among self-employed people is well documented, as are the reasons (for an overview see Kempson et al, 2000). Unsurprisingly, none of the self-employed people in the Barton Hill focus group had a private pension – they simply could not afford one from the amounts they could earn. Most of them had heard of the Stakeholder Pension, which was due to be introduced in just under a year's time, but they knew nothing about it:

> "I have heard of it, but I mean, I see pensions, I block off. I think I haven't got the money, forget it."

> "I have heard the phrase – Stakeholder Economy I think it is – but that sounds to me like one of Tony Blair's buzz-words."

The suggestion that the government should make private pensions compulsory was met with incredulity:

> "I would go on the dole. I can't afford it and I can't walk out and find any other kind of job at the age of 53."

There were two views about managing in old age. One was that they would continue to work – indeed it was part of the motivation for starting in business in the first place. The other view was that they would survive somehow:

> "I am going to hit 65 and then I am going to go on the state pension, you know, somebody or another will pay for me to survive."

These attitudes to pensions are mirrored in other recent research (Wood, 1999).

Information and advice

Two very different needs for information and advice emerged from the focus groups. Some of the Somali women had identified a possible business opportunity making videos of Somalian weddings, as women cannot be videoed or photographed in their wedding outfits by men. But they lacked the confidence to take the next step and needed both moral support and practical help to start a small business.

In contrast, the self-employed men said they had needed no assistance when they first started trading – mainly because they had never made a conscious decision to become self-employed but had started in the informal economy:

> "The thing is, I didn't actually sit down and consider when I was going to be self-employed, because I really was, to all intents and purposes, but just simply wasn't declaring it. I had no need to think about what I was going to do, or to look around for advice whether it was a good thing to do, because I was already doing it by then."

Their main needs had been for information about taxation. For example, one man went to a tax office for information and had been given leaflets he could not understand:

> "... it is still in the cupboard. I looked through it and thought 'Oh my god, this is just too much' ... basically anything I spend I just keep the receipts, I will give it to somebody else at the end to deal with."

Another had problems in his first legitimate trading year because he had over-claimed against income tax.

Only one man had consulted an accountant when he first set up in business:

"I initially consulted an accountant and he gave me some guidelines and said, 'When you are ready to come back my fee will be £350'. And I actually did take my first year's accounts back to him. But his office had closed, so I did it all myself."

In contrast, information about VAT was not an issue as no one had a turnover in excess of the VAT threshold. Similarly, no one felt that they had needed information or assistance with preparing business plans or cash-flow statements. However, this was not because they knew how to prepare them, rather that they had avoided doing so. And this remained the case, even after they had been trading for some years:

"If I've got any money I spend it, if I haven't I won't. That's the way it works basically.... That is how I chug along really."

"I have not made any business plan, I am a bit too old to map out a business plan for the next 30 years, but I am taking out adverts in the Yellow Pages and that sort of thing, so hopefully my business will pick up."

Although they had never really planned their businesses in any way, several people had continued to trade for some time. The man who considered that he was too old, at 53, to develop a business plan had, for example, been self-employed for 17 years.

In fact it became very apparent that these micro-entrepreneurs did not really see themselves as running a business at all; they merely worked for themselves. This has important implications for services that aim to provide business support in this sector.

The main needs for information and help beyond the start-up phase related to sources of finance and, again, tax matters:

"There needs to be some guidance on how best to approach financial institutions about being loaned some money, I don't know how that could be done."

"People also need tax advice as well ... it's like, when I do my tax next, that will be for the year when I had a lot of equipment stolen. I don't know how, at

the moment, to go about declaring that. Do I have to take it off my capital assets? Or do I write it in as a loss? I have no idea."

Other than the tax office, people had no idea where to go for information or advice, despite the widespread provision of services for the self-employed. The geographical isolation of Barton Hill would certainly have been a factor in this, but it also shows how such services have failed to reach poor communities and people in fairly marginal self-employment who live in them:

"There are all sorts of government help schemes, but they're more aimed at people in general lines of self-employment rather than the small businesses."

In general, young people were thought to be fairly well catered for, but not older people. As a consequence, being self-employed was likened to "walking a cliff".

Banks and financial advisers were definitely not seen as an appropriate source of advice or information. In part, this was because they were thought to be more interested in selling financial products; in part because they were thought to be too remote from the needs of very small 'life-style' businesses. In fact, what people wanted was:

"... a nice friendly face, someone to go to ... maybe someone who is independent in a way."

Meeting unmet needs

As noted above, two very different needs were identified. The Somali women would be best assisted by an organisation able to offer them moral and practical support to help them set up in business, coupled with small amounts of start-up capital if needed. Moreover, because they are Muslims, they would also require a source of finance that is non-interest bearing but that carries a fixed charge instead.

In contrast, the self-employed men recoiled at the idea of a 'hand-holding' organisation. What they most wanted was a source of accessible small loans and, when a specific need arose, practical advice and help.

Recent years have seen widespread experimentation with different approaches to micro-lending, throughout Europe and the United States (Rogaly et al, 1998; Metcalf et al, 2000; Whyley and Kempson, 2000). A lively debate has ensued about the best way of providing loans and assistance to the types of micro-entrepreneurs that exist in Barton Hill. There are arguments in favour of lending to peer groups as opposed to individual loans; in favour of loans, combined with practical support and advice; and about the most appropriate way of screening loan applications. This study shows clearly that no one style of lending can meet all the needs, even in a small, deprived community like Barton Hill.

Current provision covering Barton Hill

It is beyond the scope of this report to detail all the sources of assistance provided to small businesses (for an overview of these see the Treasury report on *Enterprise and social exclusion* [HM Treasury, 1999b] and the Bank of England's report on *Finance for small businesses in deprived communities* [Bank of England, 2000]). Instead, we concentrate on organisations that aim to tackle financial exclusion by widening access to financial services.

Bristol has three organisations offering loans and practical assistance to people setting up or operating micro-businesses. These include an office of the Prince's Trust and the Centre for Employment and Enterprise Development that has a Young Entrepreneurs' Development Fund (YEDF), both of which target young people. The third, the BEDF was set up in the early 1990s, as a lender of last resort in the most deprived areas of the city. Similar loan schemes operate in many other cities in Britain (British Bankers' Association, 1999).

The Prince's Trust is a national organisation which, since 1983, has offered finance and mentoring to young unemployed or 'under-employed' people aged between 18 and 30 who wish to become self-employed. It provides low-interest loans of up to £5,000, grants for test marketing and other special circumstances. In addition, young people are assigned an experienced, volunteer business mentor during the first three years of trading.

YEDF was set up in 1996, with support from the NatWest Charitable Trust, and provides loans, business advice and counselling to young people, especially those who live in the deprived inner-city areas of Bristol.

Young people are quite well catered for – although neither organisation has a presence within Barton Hill. Indeed, the self-employed focus group participants were aware that such schemes were available:

> "When I have seen loans like that, it is always available for people who are just starting out, who are under 28 or under 25."

They were, however, unaware of BEDF which could, in theory, have met their needs.

BEDF began making loans to small businesses in 1992, with financial support from the City Council, Business Link West and Lloyds TSB. Like many other loan schemes set up at that time, it offers subsidised loans to people who have been unable to obtain finance from any other source. All applications are made through local Enterprise Agency offices that help people to prepare the business plans on which loan decisions are based. Unlike many other 'soft loan' schemes, it requires people to provide a pro forma invoice or receipt before they will release the loan capital. The maximum loan is £5,000 for new businesses and £10,000 for existing ones. Average loans are, however, a good deal lower than the maximum. All loans are repayable over three years:

> "... but invariably we offer a loan repayment holiday at the front end, and it can be as much as six months. And because our fund is altruistic in its outlook, we give moratoriums and will listen sympathetically to requests for reduced repayments and so on."

In addition to loans, BEDF has recently begun offering a mentoring service to all successful loan applicants. BEDF had assisted 228 businesses up to the middle of 2000; its own growth has been constrained by lack of finance. This almost certainly explains why the focus group participants were unaware of its existence.

Developing current provision

Since the soft loan schemes, such as BEDF, were set up in the early 1990s, a second generation of micro-lending schemes has evolved which aim to become financially sustainable – at least as far as their loan funds are concerned. This has a number of implications for the way that they operate. First, they do not offer loans at subsidised interest rates and their experience suggests that it is access to appropriate finance rather than cost that is important to micro-entrepreneurs. Second, they seek to *manage* risk, rather than exclude potential borrowers or face high levels of bad debt.

Most, therefore, do not require business plans or collateral before they will lend, nor do they do credit checks of applicants. They also generally adopt a firm but fair approach to debt recovery and build into their lending procedures incentives for people to repay on time. All recognise the need for practical advice and support, but not all provide it directly themselves.

A review of micro-lenders identified two that were particularly appropriate for the needs identified in Barton Hill – Full Circle and Street UK. They were both invited to present details of their schemes to the select committee held at the end of the research.

The Full Circle Fund of the Women's Enterprise, Employment and Training Unit (WEETU) in Norfolk offers a peer-group lending scheme for 'emerging businesses'. This was felt to be ideally suited to the needs of the Somali women – by the women themselves, by the Somali community development worker, and also by the manager and others involved with BEDF.

Full Circle operates through lending circles of 4-6 women, who offer each other practical advice and support as well as assessing one another's loans. These circles are set up once women have been through a training scheme enabling them to test the feasibility of their business idea and have moved on to a business skills course. At the end of this they will have developed a business plan. They then have access to the loan fund and can also be helped to open a bank account, if needed.

The maximum amount that can be borrowed as a first loan is £1,000 over 20 months; the second loan £2,000 over 24 months. After that, women are encouraged to move into the commercial banking sector, although further loans can be made if necessary. The interest rate on loans is 1.5% above the rate at which Full Circle can borrow from the Charities Aid Foundation. Group peer pressure is the main method of risk management. This is exercised both before the loan is granted – there are no credit checks and loans are approved by members of the lending circle (all applications do go through a 'loan committee', but a loan can only be turned down if there are factual errors in the business plan or cashflow projections) – and also afterwards to ensure that repayments are made. If any group member defaults, others are unable to get a further loan.

The second scheme is the recently launched Street UK, which is well suited to the needs of the self-employed people who participated in the focus group, and was particularly attractive to them. Street UK launched three pilots in October 2000 but aims to operate nationally after the pilot phase. In contrast to Full Circle, its client group is anyone who has had a cash flow for three or more months. Its main client group is people operating in, or wanting to emerge from the informal economy, although it will also provide loans to immediate post-start-up micro-businesses and to micro-businesses that are fully registered but not yet bankable.

Street UK concentrates on making loans, but will offer its borrowers business support "at the customers premises and done informally". The maximum first loan is £3,000, repayable over six months. Both the amount and the term will be increased in steps with successive loans. It offers loans to mutual guarantee groups and also to individuals (who will require guarantors). Interest rates are lower for groups than for individuals, to encourage group borrowing and so reduce administration costs. In all cases, interest rates are "above the rate offered by banks to the small businesses they are keen to recruit".

What distinguishes Street UK (and its sister organisation Fundusz Mikro in Poland) from both bank lending and soft loan schemes is its approach both to risk assessment and to risk management. The granting of loans depends on an applicant having three appropriate guarantors. Where an applicant is a member of a group, other group members can act as guarantors. In such cases, however, the strength and nature of the relationships between group members are also assessed. Street UK does not require a business plan or collateral. Instead, loan officers decide how much they are willing to lend by discussing and assessing the applicant's motivation and entrepreneurial skills, the viability of their business and cash flow position. Credit checks may be made, but a poor credit history does not necessarily preclude the granting of a loan – each application is assessed individually.

Both Full Circle and Street UK were keen to assist developments both in Bristol and elsewhere. Indeed, Full Circle have a package, including manuals and on-site training for one to two weeks, that can be bought by other organisations. In discussion, both during and following the select committee, there was widespread support for taking things forward and building on the expertise of BEDF. The manager of BEDF was especially keen:

> "There are lots of super ideas now, which I'd love to explore to see how we can weld them onto, not just BEDF, but to a one-stop-shop type of thing. I'd love all budding entrepreneurs to have one door they can knock on."

7

Moving forward

Earlier chapters have addressed different aspects of financial exclusion, but all the discussions – in the focus groups, the select committees and interviews with local providers – showed clearly that needs do not come in neat compartments. One of the clearest messages from the research was the need for a 'one-stop shop approach' to meeting unmet needs.

There were, however, some other important aspects to any future development. First, needs would best be met by city-wide and national provision – not purely local organisations. Second, and just as important, these city-wide and national providers need to have a local presence in deprived areas like Barton Hill. Third, there needs to be a partnership approach between commercial companies and providers with a local presence. Fourth, it is important to build on existing provision and expertise and to involve local residents. Finally, solutions need to be found that are sustainable in the long term.

One-stop shop

The need for a one-stop shop approach was a recurrent theme in the discussions at the end of the select committee of local representatives. In the first instance, this would encompass personal savings and loans, loans for micro-businesses, financial literacy, financial information and advice and business support. It might, at a later date, develop access to insurance as well.

It was also apparent that local residents, themselves, would favour a one-stop shop. On the one hand, they wanted simple, unbundled, financial products that would allow them to keep tight control over their money. For example, they did not want credit facilities tied to a bank

account; instead they preferred to have a bank account they could not overdraw and have separate access to cash loans, repayable in fixed amounts. On the other hand, it was equally clear that their needs were frequently closely linked. For example, they wanted to be able to access financial information and advice when they were taking out a financial product. They liked the idea of using savings to gain access to low-cost loans as with credit unions or the *New Horizons* savings and loans scheme. Also, the self-employed often made little distinction between personal and business finances – quite possibly to their detriment.

Banks and other mainstream financial institutions have recognised this interconnection of needs. Since de-regulation in the 1980s, most offer their customers a wide range of different financial services, including transactional banking, mortgages, consumer credit, and insurance – both for personal and business needs. But these developments have not encompassed the needs of people, like those in Barton Hill, who live on low incomes.

In contrast, the alternative financial service provision that exists to meet the needs of poor people is generally fragmented. This applies as much in the not-for-profit sector as it does in the commercial world of door-to-door moneylenders and home service insurance companies. The select committee and interviews with local representatives showed that, although they form a close network, they had not previously appreciated the need for a joined-up approach to their service delivery:

"It's really clear that there's really strong linkages, not only from micro-enterprises – private ones and social economy ones –

but between domestic and micro-enterprise finance, between benefit and debt advice and personal [finance] and business advice ... there's linkages all over the place."

There was a recognition that the vagaries of funding have encouraged voluntary sector organisations to concentrate on meeting very specific needs, and placed them in potential conflict as they compete for limited grant aid:

"Do you think that we often spend too much time fighting over a small cake, whereas if we all combined together we'd get a much larger cake to share between us?"

City-wide and national provision

It was equally clear from both residents and local representatives that unmet needs for financial services are best met by national or city-wide organisations. Four main reasons were identified by them.

First, local residents articulated a clear desire to be part of mainstream financial service provision. They wanted financial services that were appropriate to life on a low, but fluctuating, income. So they wanted the option of having fairly limited financial products while they were out of work but to be able to scale things up when they were in work. The last thing they wanted was to have to keep changing providers in order to get access to appropriate financial services.

Second, Barton Hill, like most other poor neighbourhoods, has a very high population turnover. As a consequence, local residents need access to financial services that are portable. The turnover in local authority housing is too high to develop solutions just for Barton Hill, only to find that 20% of the local tenants have moved out the following year. Residents would then be right back where they started, because they have moved into another area of Bristol that has no provision.

Third, Barton Hill only has a relatively small population and, while credit unions have been set up in such small communities, this is no longer seen as the way forward for a sustainable credit

union movement. It involves too much duplication of effort and results in organisations that are severely constrained in the services they can provide. Fourth, and linked to this, is the fact that any form of one-stop shop provision would simply not be viable.

Local outlets

At the same time, it was also quite clear that both national and city-wide provision requires local outlets if it is to combat financial exclusion in deprived neighbourhoods. There are two main reasons for this.

First, there is a need to provide physical access. Barton Hill, like so many deprived neighbourhoods, is cut off geographically from the city centre. The distance, as the crow flies, is not great, but the railway line and canal traversing the area mean that actual journeys are a good deal longer. Added to which the cost of public transport (£1.60 return on the bus for an adult) means that local residents, many of whom have small children, do not often go into the city centre.

Second, there are psychological barriers to the use of financial services that are every bit as great as the physical ones. The focus groups with local residents identified a widespread mistrust of financial services providers and a general disengagement from financial services provision. Although they liked the various solutions described to them in person in the select committee, it became clear that much needs to be done to encourage take up. As one bank representative commented:

"From talking to the residents earlier, there is a level of interest, but whether that will actually be turned into engagement and use, I don't know."

Local one-stop access can potentially be provided in two ways. There could be one city-wide organisation that has local offices. Alternatively, local outlets could provide a gateway on behalf of a range of city-wide services that operate in close collaboration. Such a gateway service would act as an agency for other service providers and not merely as a referral organisation.

Partnerships

Local partnerships were seen as a way of developing national and Bristol-wide services to tackle financial exclusion that have a local presence in Barton Hill and other deprived neighbourhoods in the city.

The residents were attracted to transactional banking services being delivered through local Post Offices. As we have noted in Chapter 3, they liked the idea of being part of mainstream banking, but preferred dealing with the Post Office. They not only found local Post Offices a good deal easier to get to than bank and building society branches, but also found them much more approachable and in tune with the needs of people living on a low income. This augers well, both for the Universal Bank proposals and for the future of banking agency arrangements with the Post Office.

Partnerships were also seen as the way forward in other areas. In particular, they were thought to be the best way of developing a one-stop shop service to meet the needs for savings, loans and financial literacy – both for individuals and for people who are self-employed. Organisations such as the Portsmouth Area Regeneration Trust were seen as the most appropriate way forward. Banks and other financial institutions were acknowledged as having expertise and resources they could contribute, but lacking credibility with people on the margins of financial services.

One banker described how they were developing new products to "be more inclusive than we are", including a basic bank account and a low-cost, basic household contents insurance. But, he also recognised that there were limits to what they could achieve alone:

> "I think we [the banks] are realists and we get to a point where I would describe it as, we're no longer the people to do the job, either by virtue of our size or the way we operate."

A second banker also saw partnerships with local organisations as the best way of tackling financial exclusion:

> "Are there ways of demystifying [financial services] that [local] organisations can help us with? ... Now is there something we can do within this local community to test working with trusted organisations who can help us through [the mistrust]?"

Indeed, two of the main high-street banks were keen to work with local organisations in Bristol to explore ways of widening access to financial services.

Most cities, like Bristol, will have some provision in the voluntary sector that is trying to reach people who are financially excluded: a credit union, a soft loan scheme, literacy and numeracy initiatives or advice agencies. But these are invariably over-stretched and are unable to respond to further needs, as the staff involved in running them commented:

> "Credit unions, for instance, do have limited capacity at the moment, in terms of how much they can lend."

> "That need for micro-funding for small business is crucial. We've actually had to limit our lending because we just cannot cope with the demand."

Building on local provision and expertise

There was no appetite among local representatives for starting from scratch to find local solutions to financial exclusion. Indeed, there was a strongly held view that services should:

* learn from experience in other localities;
* build on existing local services;
* involve local residents in the process.

There was unanimous agreement that the best way forward is to adapt solutions that have been tried and tested elsewhere to meet local needs. One of the bankers who had been involved in developing community finance initiatives in other localities had this advice to offer:

> "I suppose that what I'm saying is, don't go for something new for the sake of it, because it's real hard work. But equally reject or shy away from it if it's not right for the job."

It was equally clear that the local credit union and

soft loan scheme were keen to play a part in developing a more joined-up approach to combating financial exclusion. There was, for example, considerable interest in the way that PART has built on local services. Whether it is more appropriate for these local services to coalesce or to develop close collaborative arrangements would need to be discussed.

Moreover, experience elsewhere has identified a real need for a strong local organisation that can work with national bodies, such as the banks, to spearhead the development of joint services. In the case of PART, Portsmouth Housing Association took on this role, working in partnership with Lloyds TSB who provided resources, including the secondment of a senior member of staff:

> "We needed that base, that local expertise, to make sure the whole thing could operate … I believe it's absolutely crucial that you have that strong anchor to make something like this to go ahead."

Just as importantly, local residents themselves need to play an active role in determining the services that should be developed to meet their needs. As one of the bankers at the select committee commented:

> "You've obviously got the residents involved and you're using them, in my view, in exactly the right way."

Sustainability

Local representatives were only too well aware of the dangers of developing new services without a long-term plan for achieving financial sustainability. The hand-to-mouth grant culture was generally believed to have held back service development in the past. Equally, in the course of the interviews with local voluntary sector organisations, there was criticism of the way that government and EU initiatives (for example the New Deal for Communities) come and go, and fail to establish services that survive the initiatives.

Consequently, there was much interest in establishing a Bristol-wide not-for-profit financial services provider, offering savings and loans facilities to both individuals and micro-businesses on a self-financing basis. Any grant aid would then be concentrated on developing financial

literacy, financial information and advice and business support services.

Taking stock and moving forward

Local residents and local representatives were of one mind. The process used to understand local needs and identify ways of improving access to financial services had been a valuable one.

The residents felt that, perhaps for the first time, they had actually had an important role in determining how things might develop in the future. The focus groups had enabled them to voice their criticisms of financial service provision and they welcomed the opportunity to hear at first hand from people designing financial services intended to meet their needs. They proved to be skilful cross-examiners in the select committee and felt a degree of optimism about future provision. The whole exercise proved, beyond doubt, the value of giving a voice to local people, recruited on the doorstep.

The local representatives equally valued having the chance to learn about and discuss a wide range of different ways of combating financial exclusion. But for them it was only a start:

> "… we've heard about loads of things today, loads of opportunities. There's some that you can straight away say, 'Yes that's probably required in most low-income areas'…. I think there's other, bigger things that require quite a big commitment to get off the ground. It seems as the day goes on, it becomes all the more clear that we need to set up some means of sifting through these ideas and deciding which we're going to run with."

There was great enthusiasm for taking things forward. Both local residents and local representatives said that they would like to be involved as the project enters its developmental stage. Two high-street banks have expressed an interest in working with them to develop services that meet local needs and have a wider applicability.

Taking things forward will, however, require more than enthusiasm. Experience in Portsmouth (PART), Salford (Moneyline) and Easterhouse, where banks and others have worked together to set up community-based banking facilities, does provide a number of useful pointers. First, it is important that there is a genuine partnership between national providers (such as banks) and local organisations. There is, however, likely to be a huge disparity in scale between the partners, and consequently a lead organisation needs to be designated locally. The local authority, a housing association, or a local regeneration/development body have all played this role in other partnerships. The most likely candidate in Bristol is probably the Bristol Regeneration Partnership.

Second, one or more people will need to be appointed who will have day-to-day responsibility for ensuring that things move forward and that planned services actually materialise. They would be responsible for arranging visits to projects elsewhere to obtain practical information that can be distilled and applied to the situation in Bristol.

Third, local people should continue to be involved in the discussion, development and implementation of initiatives.

One of the local representatives summed up the overall approach:

> "I don't want people to fall through nets. I don't want us to reinvent wheels, but I do want us to design new wheels. And I'd like to see that things that we design for Barton Hill are exportable to other parts of Bristol and, hopefully, to other parts of the country."

References

Bank of England (2000) *Finance for small businesses in deprived communities*, London: Bank of England, Domestic Finance Division.

BBA Enterprises Limited (1999) *You and proving your identity*, London: British Bankers' Association.

Bevan, J., Clark, G., Banerji, N. and Hakim, C. (1989) *Barriers to business start-up: A study of the flow into and out of self-employment*, London: Department of Employment.

Blanchflower, D.G. and Oswald, A.J. (1991a) *What makes an entrepreneur?*, Economics Discussion Paper No 125, Oxford: Institute of Economics and Statistics, University of Oxford.

Blanchflower, D.G. and Oswald, A.J. (1991b) *Self-employment and Mrs Thatcher's enterprise culture*, Discussion Paper No 30, London: Centre for Economic Performance, London School of Economics and Political Science.

British Bankers' Association (1999) *Micro credit in the UK: An inventory of schemes for business supported by banks*, London: British Bankers' Association.

Burrows, B. (1999) *Living in a homeless hostel: You wouldn't credit it!*, Money Advice Scotland.

Conaty, P. and Mayo, E. (undated) *A commitment to people and place: The case for community development credit unions*, New Economics Foundation.

DETR (Department of the Environment, Transport and the Regions) (1998) 'Prescott announces £800 million New Deal for deprived communities', Press Release, 15 September.

DfEE (Department for Education and Employment) (2000a) *Adult Financial Literacy Advisory Group: Report to the Secretary of State for Education and Employment*, London: DfEE.

DfEE (2000b) *Financial capability through personal finance education: Guidance for schools at Key Stages 1 and 2*, London: DfEE.

DfEE (2000c) *Financial capability through personal finance education: Guidance for schools at Key Stages 3 and 4*, London: DfEE.

Drakeford, M. and Sachdev, D. (forthcoming) 'Financial exclusion and debt redemption', *Critical Social Policy*.

Feloy, M. and Payne, D. (1999) *People, communities and credit unions*, Birmingham: Birmingham Credit Union Development Agency Limited.

Finance and Leasing Association (2000) *Guide to credit scoring*, London: Finance and Leasing Authority.

Ford, J. and Kempson, E. (1997) *Bridging the gap: Safety-nets for mortgage borrowers*, York: Centre for Housing Policy.

HM Treasury (1999a) *Access to financial services: National strategy for neighbourhood renewal*, Report of Policy Action Team 14, London: HM Treasury.

HM Treasury (1999b) *Enterprise and social exclusion: National strategy for neighbourhood renewal*, Report of Policy Action Team 3, London: HM Treasury.

HM Treasury (1999c) *Credit unions of the future*, London: HM Treasury.

Jones, P. (1998) *Towards sustainable credit union development*, Manchester: Association of British Credit Unions Limited.

Kempson, E. (1998) *Savings and low income and ethnic minority households*, London: Personal Investment Authority.

Kempson, E. and Jones, T. (2000) *Banking without branches*, London: British Bankers' Association.

Kempson, E. and Whyley, C. (1998a) *Benchmarking in microlending: UK country report*, PFRC Working Paper, Bristol: Personal Finance Research Centre, University of Bristol.

Kempson, E. and Whyley, C. (1998b) *Access to current accounts*, London: British Bankers' Association.

Kempson, E. and Whyley, C. (1999) *Kept out or opted out?: Understanding and combating financial exclusion*, Bristol/York: The Policy Press/Joseph Rowntree Foundation.

Kempson, E. and Whyley, C. (2000) *Extortionate credit in the UK*, London: Department of Trade and Industry.

Kempson, E., Bryson, A. and Rowlingson, K. (1994) *Hard times?: How poor families make ends meet*, London: Policy Studies Institute.

Kempson, E., Ford, J. and Quilgars, D. (1999) *Unsafe safety-nets*, York: Centre for Housing Policy.

Kempson, E., Whyley, C., Caskey, J. and Collard, S. (2000) *In or out? Financial exclusion: a literature and research review*, Consumer Research Report 3, London: Financial Services Authority.

Loumidis, J. and Middleton, S. (2000) *A cycle of disadvantage? Financial exclusion in childhood*, Consumer Research Report 4, London: Financial Services Authority.

Metcalfe, H., Crowley, T., Anderson, T. and Bainton, C. (2000) *From unemployment to self-employment: The role of micro-finance*, London: International Labour Office.

National Consumer Council (1997) *In the bank's bad books: How the banking code of practice works for customers in hardship*, London: National Consumer Council.

New Deal for Communities Bristol (1999) *Community at Heart*, Bristol: New Deal for Communities Bristol.

Noctor, M., Stoney, S. and Stradling, S. (1992) *Financial literacy: A discussion of concepts and competences of financial literacy for its introduction into young people's learning*, National Foundation for Education Research.

Office of Fair Trading (1999) *The consumer survey*, Report No OFT 255d, London: Office of Fair Trading.

Rogaly, B., Fisher, T. and Mayo, E. (1998) *Poverty, social exclusion, microfinance in Britain*, Oxford: Oxfam.

Rowlingson, K. (1994) *Moneylenders and their customers*, London: Policy Studies Institute.

SEU (Social Exclusion Unit) (1998) *Bringing Britain together: A national strategy for neighbourhood renewal*, London: Cabinet Office.

SEU (2001) *New commitment to neighbourhood renewal*, London: Cabinet Office.

Speak, S. and Graham, S. (2000) *Service not included: Social implications of private sector service restructuring in marginalised neighbourhoods*, Bristol/York: The Policy Press/Joseph Rowntree Foundation.

Whyley, C. (1998) *Risky business: The personal and financial costs of small business failure*, London: Policy Studies Institute.

Whyley, C. and Kempson, E. (2000) *Banks and micro-lending: Support, co-operation and learning*, Hamburg: Institut fur Finanzdienstleistungen.

Whyley, C., Collard, S. and Kempson, E. (2000) *Saving and borrowing: Use of the Social Fund Budgeting Loan scheme and community credit unions*, London: Department of Social Security.

Wood, C. (1999) *Pensions for all*, Peterborough: Pearl Assurance.